Kisses on Paper

Kisses on Paper

Edited by Jill Dawson

faber and faber
BOSTON • LONDON

First published in the United States in 1995 by
Faber and Faber, Inc., 50 Cross Street, Winchester,
MA 01890. Originally published in the
United Kingdom in 1994 by Virago Press Limited,
42–43 Gloucester Crescent, London NW1 7PD.

ISBN 0-571-19864-3

A CIP catalogue record for this book
is available from the Library of Congress.

Jacket design by the Senate.
Jacket shows 'Repose' by John White Alexander
(1856–1915).
The Metropolitan Museum of Art,
Anonymous Gift, 1980.

Printed in Great Britain.

For Karen – 'Be happy; be it as much as you deserve it;
it is my entire heart that speaks to you'

– Empress Josephine to Napoleon Bonaparte, 1810

CONTENTS

ACKNOWLEDGEMENTS

I am indebted to Andrew Graham once again, for his considerable contribution to *Kisses on Paper* in terms of time, research and many hours of discussion in the British Library. I'd like to thank Melanie Silgardo at Virago for the invitation, and for her editorial expertise and encouragement, and all those who gave permission for letters to be included in this book, with particular thanks to those writers who let me see recent love letters: Suniti Namjoshi, Gillian Hanscombe, Felly Simmonds and Mary Meigs.

I'm grateful to those who lent me books, to Adrian Whittle and Liane, and to those who suggested or translated letters – Kate, Stella, Jamie McKendrick and Alison Hennegan. I am most grateful of all to the staff of Wentworth Nursery, notably Janice, Jill, Frances and Carolyn Maples, for providing me with the necessary time and peace of mind to put this book together, and to Stewart for support and encouragement.

Kisses on Paper

INTRODUCTION

'This is a sort of love letter I suppose. Odd that I should be writing you a love letter after all these years –' wrote Vita Sackville-West, in some surprise, to Violet Trefusis in 1950, thirty years after their love affair ended. What quality is it that whisks an ordinary letter into a letter of love? Mary Wordsworth, writing to her husband William in 1812, has no doubts at all – a love letter, she declares, is nothing less than the 'breathing of thy inmost heart upon paper'.

Of course, apart from a few exceptions, this 'breathing of the inmost heart' was intended only for the eyes (or ears) of the beloved. The nineteenth-century French writer George Sand vehemently urged her lover, Alfred de Musset, to keep letters from her safely locked in a casket. She warned that 'death can surprise one at any minute, and one never knows what hand will rifle one's drawers as soon as one's eyes are closed'. Most contemporary writers, understandably, share her desire for their drawers to remain unrifled, and in the main this collection is of love letters discovered or published after the writer's death. (In Sand's case her protestations may have been disingenuous. Soon after her romance with de Musset she published a novel full of intimate revelations. De Musset also milked their relationship for all it was worth in his writing, and both agreed to have their love letters published in their lifetime, to the delight of a scandalised public.)

Simone de Beauvoir was more prudent. She maintained that her love letters to Jean-Paul Sartre had been lost, and they were not found until after her death in 1986, by her adopted daughter, Sylvie Le Bon de Beauvoir, in a cupboard in de Beauvoir's own apartment. Perhaps de Beauvoir had anticipated the furore their publication was to cause. One reviewer described the letters as having 'more than a whiff of *Les Liaisons dangereuses*' about them. Whatever the controversy (and the letters do lay bare a woman with remarkable sexual and emotional energy, jumping through hoops to pursue simultaneous love affairs with Sartre, and other men and women), the letters flesh out, rather than reduce, the picture of Simone de Beauvoir we have from her other writing. As Sylvie Le Bon de Beauvoir says, you 'certainly hear her voice in them, its most fleeting along with its most constant tones: her true, living voice'.

De Beauvoir's case illustrates another point: to be able to find and publish love letters, somebody somewhere must value them, or *value the letter writer*. This simple fact accounts for many gaps and losses. Whilst Mileva Marić, sweetheart and wife of Albert Einstein, carefully preserved all his love letters to her, he did not afford hers the same concern, and of hundreds written, only eleven remain. Love letters by Black writers, writers of the Harlem Renaissance, Native American writers, proved elusive despite many enquiries, although it's hard to believe that none survives.

Love letters by 'ordinary' women – that is neither writers nor figures in public life – tend to have been saved because the women were caught up in singular circumstances. Edith Thompson was put on trial with her young lover Frederick Bywaters in 1922 for the murder of her husband. Her love letters were used in court as evidence against her; they remain in the British Library, the fascinating testimony of a fanciful, capricious woman who, from her own account, seems unlikely to have intended Bywaters to kill her husband, and was probably hanged not for that but for expressing a wish to do so, and for adultery.

Another accused adulteress, Anne Boleyn, penned an amazingly dignified letter to her accuser, King Henry VIII, given her circumstances (she was awaiting trial in the Tower of London). It could hardly be described as a love letter at all, except that it follows the form perfectly: 'If ever I have found favour in your sight, if ever the name of Anne Boleyn hath been pleasing in your ears . . .'. There is some dispute about the letter – it may well be a fake, as the handwriting does not correspond with other examples of Boleyn's writing, but nevertheless it demonstrates a skill in the *art* of the love letter which is especially evident in women writing letters of rejection. Queen Elizabeth I, turning down a suitor, only once betrays her irritation at his proposal, and her astute political assessment of his motives: 'I could never have believed that anyone would have spoken to me of nuptials at a time when I ought to think of nothing but sorrow for the death of my father.'

That women have a reputation for excelling in letter writing doesn't mean that some wouldn't appreciate a little help. Poets Suniti Namjoshi and Gillian Hanscombe, initially surprised at an invitation to run a 'love letter writing workshop', were further astonished at the turn-out. But after all, many of the most unlikely candidates for romance or creative writing have attempted a love letter, and longing to write a better one is not unreasonable, although it might threaten our wish to believe – like Vita Sackville-West – that love letters should magically write themselves.

Despair, desolation and longing are the food of love – letters in the sections **Rejection** and **Desolation** far outnumbered those found for

Invitation or **Consummation**, perhaps for the obvious reason that 'consummating' is more time-consuming than pining. Love letters of explicit sexual desire were somewhat thin on the ground, too; one exception being Anaïs Nin's letters to Henry Miller, which are (predictably) scorching. **Temptation and Frustration** was another category which was bursting at the seams; many lovers wrote a stream of desperate letters leading up to their elopement or a marriage which was being thwarted by some other party. Of course, once the longed-for union was achieved, the letters usually dried up, and the reader is left wondering whether it was all worth it in the end. Long silences or a complete absence of love letters are the legacies of lovers who were never parted – one can only imagine the letters of, for instance, Gertrude Stein and Alice B. Toklas, who claimed never to have spent a day apart since first meeting.

Occasionally writers of some standing (Katherine Mansfield and Anne Sexton come to mind) prove themselves susceptible to possession by the same infantile, schmaltzy demon that writes Valentine cards. If you want your own love letters to avoid the same fate, it may be noted that this appears to occur particularly in the throes of **Adulation**. . . . Some lovers are convinced that love letters are overrated; Jane Welsh Carlyle tells Thomas Carlyle in 1826: 'these kisses on paper are scarce worth keeping. You gave me one on my neck that night you were in such good humour, and one on my lips on some forgotten occasion, that I would not part with for a hundred thousand paper ones.'

Other anthologies of love letters exist, and I consulted many while working on this compilation. They told – in a phrase which, at the time of writing, has a certain topicality – 'an entirely heterosexual love story'. An anthology of letters by women only, far from being lopsided, teases out many women who have been overshadowed by their lovers' reputations; and instead of merely worshipping at the shrine of romantic, sexual love, as our culture entreats us to do, casts a wider net. It avoids dreary classifications and boxes, forcing an editor into prurient and irrelevant concerns – having to decide if a passionate friendship between women was 'lesbian' or not, or whether an unconsummated affair was 'sexual' in nature. . . . How on earth could one honestly say that the love Colette felt for Marguerite Moreno, a love which lasted fifty-four years, was only a shade of love, not the *real* love of, for instance, a famous couple like Joséphine and Napoleon?

Is there a difference between the love letters of women and those of men? Probably not, but the assumption in mixed anthologies seems to be that there is. Anthologists of the past were able to write without a hint of embarrassment that 'Male forms the Variety, the Female the Species. The Wave advances, the Ocean remains constant. This principle applied to our love letters, goes to explain the fact that it is the man who writes the first letter, and the woman who answers him' (C.H. Charles, editor of *Love Letters of Great Men and Women*). *Male forms the variety, female the species* – women, as ever, even when they are doing something as straightforward as writing a letter, being cast in the role of deviant from the norm, or lesser. Here it is possible to perceive women letter writers as both wave and ocean: crashing, retreating, advancing, responding or remaining constant – according not to the dictates of their sex but to the dictates of mood, feeling and predilection.

Jill Dawson, 1994

INVITATION:
'Will you admit me now?'

VIRGINIA WOOLF (1882–1941)
England

Innovative and daring English novelist and essayist, author of – amongst other works – To the Lighthouse, The Waves *and the famous essay* A Room of One's Own. *Leading member of the influential Bloomsbury Group, which included her sister, the painter Vanessa Bell.*

She was married to Leonard Woolf in 1912. Her affair with Vita Sackville-West began in 1925, shortly after this letter was sent, and continued, as an intense and central friendship, up until Woolf's death by suicide in 1941. (See also ***Declaration, Consummation, Desolation****, and Vita Sackville-West's letter to Violet Trefusis in* ***Celebration****.) Woolf's novel* Orlando *(1928), dedicated to Sackville-West and discussed often in their correspondence, has been called 'the most charming and longest love letter in history'.*

To Vita Sackville-West

52 Tavistock Square
Thursday [10 December]

My dear Vita,
Would Tuesday afternoon suit you?
Should I stay till Friday or Saturday?
Should Leonard come and fetch me back?
Should you mind if I only brought one dressing gown?
Should I be a nuisance if I had breakfast in bed?

Berg

JANE CLAIRMONT (1798–1879)
England

Jane Clairmont (also known as Claire or Clara) was the half-sister of Mary Shelley, daughter of the second Mrs Godwin. In 1816 Clairmont spent the summer with Mary and Percy Shelley and the poet Byron, with whom she fell instantly and dramatically in love.

The following letter offers a contradiction to the prevailing myth of Clairmont as a hysteric; it suggests a bold personality, efficiently organising an illicit meeting with Byron 'so that the slightest suspicion may not be excited'.

Byron was married at the time. He fathered Clairmont's illegitimate daughter, Allegra (born 1817). (See also the letter from Byron's wife on page 101).

To Lord Byron

(1815)

You bid me write short to you and I have much to say. You also bade me believe that it was a fancy which made me cherish an attachment for you. It cannot be a fancy since you have been for the last year the object upon which every solitary moment led me to muse.

I do not expect you to love me, I am not worthy of your love. I feel you are superior, yet much to my surprise, more to my happiness, you betrayed passions I had believed no longer alive in your bosom. Shall I also have to ruefully experience the want of happiness? Shall I reject it when it is offered? I may appear to you imprudent, vicious; my opinions detestable, my theory depraved; but one thing, at least, time shall show you that I love gently and with affection, that I am incapable of anything approaching to the feeling of revenge or malice; I do assure you, your future will shall be mine, and everything you shall do or say, I shall not question.

Have you then any objection to the following plan? On Thursday Evening we may go out of town together by some stage or mail about the distance of ten or twelve miles. There we shall be free and unknown; we can return early the following morning. I have arranged every thing here so that the slightest suspicion may not be excited. Pray do so with your people.

Will you admit me for two moments to settle with you where? Indeed I will not stay an instant after you tell me to go. Only so much may be said and done in a short time by an interview which writing cannot effect. Do what you will, or go where you will, refuse to see me and behave unkindly, I shall never forget you. I shall ever remember the gentleness of your manners and the wild originality of your countenance. Having been once seen, you are not to be forgotten. Perhaps this is the last time I shall ever address you. Once more, then, let me assure you that I am not ungrateful. In all things have you acted most honourably, and I am only provoked that the awkwardness of my manner and something like timidity has hitherto prevented my expressing it to you personally.

Clara Clairmont

Will you admit me now as I wait in Hamilton Place for your answer?

GEORGE SAND (1804–76)
France

George Sand (real name Aurore Dupin), the famous nineteenth-century French novelist, was married at eighteen to the Baron Dudevant, but soon found conjugal life boring. She took up with a young writer, Jules Sandeau, from whom she took her pen name. A string of love affairs followed, the most celebrated being with the French poet Alfred de Musset.

As they travelled through Europe together in 1834, de Musset, an addict of the 'Emerald Poison', absinthe, became desperately ill. Sand found him a Venetian doctor, Pietro Pagello, but at de Musset's bedside she felt herself passionately attracted to the young man, and in less than an hour she wrote the following extraordinary letter. Described as a 'burning hymn to Eros' by her shocked biographers, the letter is a strange cocktail of lust and repulsion. Sand noted in her diary that she gave her declaration to 'the stupid Pagello', and although they briefly became lovers after de Musset's recovery, she soon tired of him. *(See also **Rejection**.)*

To Pietro Pagello

Venice, July 10th, 1834

Pietro Pagello has given this manuscript by George Sand to Antonietta Segato.
En Moree
Born under different skies we have neither the same thoughts nor the same language – have we, perhaps, hearts that resemble one another?

The mild and cloudy climate from which I come has left me with gentle and melancholy impressions; what passions has the generous sun that has bronzed your brow given you? I know how to love and how to suffer, and you, what do you know of love?

The ardour of your glances, the violent clasp of your arms, the fervour of your desire, tempt me and frighten me. I do not know whether to combat your passion or to share it. One does not love like this in my country; beside you I am no more than a pale statue that regards you with desire, with trouble, with astonishment. I do not know if you truly love me, I shall never know it. You can scarcely speak a few words of my language and I do not know enough of yours to enter into these subtle questions. Perhaps, even if I knew perfectly the language that you speak, I should not be able to make myself understood. The place where we have lived, the people that have taught us, are, doubtless, the reason that we have ideas, sentiments and needs, inexplicable one to the other. My feeble nature and your fiery temperament must produce very different thoughts. You must be ignorant of, or despise, the thousand trivial sufferings that so disturb me; you must laugh at what makes me weep. Perhaps you even do not know what tears are. Would you be for me a support or a master? Would you console me for the evils that I have endured before meeting you? Do you understand why I am sad? Do you understand compassion, patience, friendship? Perhaps you have been brought up in the idea that women have no souls. Do you think that they have? You are neither a Christian nor a Mussulman, neither civilised nor a barbarian – are you a man? What is there in that masculine bosom, behind that superb brow, those leonine eyes? Do you ever have a nobler, finer thought, a fraternal pious sentiment? When you sleep, do you dream that you are flying towards Heaven? When men wrong you do you still trust in God? Shall I be your companion or your slave? Do you desire me or love me? When your passion is satisfied will you thank me? When I have made you happy, will you know how to tell me so? Do you know what I am and does it trouble you not to know it? Am I for you an unknown being who must be sought for and dreamt of, or am I in your eyes a woman like those that fatten in harems? In your eyes, in which I think to see a divine spark, is there nothing but a lust such as these women inspire? Do you know that desire of the soul that time does not quench, that no excess deadens or wearies? When your mistress sleeps in your arms, do you stay awake to watch over her, to pray to God and to weep? Do the pleasures of love leave you breathless and brutalised or do they throw you into a divine ecstasy? Does your soul overcome your body when you leave the bosom of her whom you love? Ah, when I shall observe you withdrawn quiet, shall I know if you are thoughtful or at rest? When your glance is languishing will it be tenderness or lassitude? Perhaps you realise that I do not know you and that you do not know me. I know neither your past life, nor your character, nor what the men that know you think of you. Perhaps you are the first, perhaps the last among them. I love you without knowing if I can esteem you, I love you because you please me, and perhaps some day I shall be forced to hate you. If you were a man of my country, I should question you and you would understand me. But perhaps I should be still more unhappy, for you would mislead me. As it is, at least you will not deceive me, you will make no vain promises and false vows. You will love me as you understand love, as you can love. What I have sought for in vain in others, I shall not, perhaps, find in you, but I can always believe that you possess it. Those looks, those caresses of love that have always lied to me in others, you will allow me to interpret as I wish, without adding deceitful words to them. I shall be able to interpret your reveries and fill your silences with eloquence. I shall give to your actions the intentions that I wish them to have. When you look at me tenderly, I shall believe that your soul is gazing at mine; when you glance at heaven, I shall believe that your mind turns towards the eternity from which it sprang. Let us remain thus, do not learn my language, and I shall not look for, in yours, words to express my doubts and my fears. I want to be ignorant of what you do with your life and what part you play among your fellow-men. I do not even want to know your name. Hide your soul from me that I may always believe it to be beautiful.

Translated by Félix Decori

ANNE GUDIS (*b.* 1923)
USA

In 1942, at the age of nineteen, Anne Gudis of Newark, New Jersey, began writing to Samuel Kramer, a young soldier undergoing his basic training in Alabama, after a friend gave her his name and address. The correspondence developed into a choppy romance, and the couple managed a few meetings before Sammy was posted overseas.

Women making invitations are unusual. It seems that Samuel may have considered Anne's forthright personality 'tawdry and garish' (in the words of one of her friends), and over the three years of their correspondence she was frequently irritated by the tone of his letters to her. A year later, after two failed meetings, she wrote him a rude rejection which was published in the magazine Yank *and brought Anne a great deal of adverse publicity and attention. At the end of the war the couple married. (See also* ***Rejection*** *.)*

To Samuel Kramer

Newark, May [?], 1942

Hi, Sammy:
How are you? I bet you think I am awfully bold calling you by your first name when we don't even know each other. Well, that's where you are mistaken. I do know you. Of course, I have never met you personally, but I've heard so much about you I feel that I know you anyway. Where did I hear about you, in this remote New Jersey town? Ah, that's a secret. Of course you will find out soon, that is, if you answer this letter.

I know you aren't in the Army long, so how is Uncle Sam treating you. Are you used to the heat? I bet it's terrific compared with that little town from upstate NY that you come from. I know I shouldn't belittle Ithaca, because, after all, it is your home town.

I'll bet you are anxious to know all about me, aren't you? Looks, shape, brains, etc. Well I'm an awful tease, so I'll wait until I hear from you before I divulge my information.

Hoping to hear from you soon. I remain.

Anne Gudis

EMILY DICKINSON (1830–86)
USA

The great American poet Emily Dickinson lived all her life in Amherst, Massachusetts. Owing to bad advice from the critic Thomas Wentworth Higginson, to whom she sent some of her poems, she was not published until after her death. Even then, readers were not able to appreciate her poetry as it had been written until 1955, with the publication of Thomas Johnson's edition of her work, which firmly established her reputation as a poet of dazzling power.

Dickinson had a close friendship with Susan Gilbert, who later married her brother Austin. The relationship between the two women produced many astonishing love letters from Dickinson, revealing her as passionate, witty and candid. (See also ***Adulation, Consummation*** *and* ***Celebration****.)*

To Susan Gilbert (Dickinson)

about 6 February 1852

Will you let me come dear Susie – looking just as I do, my dress soiled and worn, my grand old apron, and my hair – Oh Susie, time would fail me to enumerate my appearance, yet I love you just as dearly as if I was e'er so fine, so you wont care, will you? I am so glad dear Susie – that our hearts are always clean, and always neat and lovely, so not to be ashamed. I have been hard at work this morning, and I ought to be working now – but I cannot deny myself the luxury of a minute or two with you.

The dishes may wait dear Susie – and the uncleared table stand, *them* I have always with me, but you, I have 'not always' – *why* Susie, Christ hath saints *manie* – and I have *few*, but thee – the angels shant have Susie – no – no no!

Vinnie is sewing away like a *fictitious* seamstress, and I half expect some knight will arrive at the door, confess himself a *nothing* in presence of her loveliness, and present his heart and hand as the only vestige of him worthy to be refused.

Vinnie and I have been talking about growing old, today. Vinnie thinks *twenty* must be a fearful position for one to occupy – I tell her I dont care if I am young or not, had as lief be thirty, and you, as most anything else. Vinnie expresses her sympathy at my 'sere and yellow leaf' and resumes her work, dear Susie, tell me how *you* feel – ar'nt there days in one's life when to be old dont seem a thing so sad –

I do feel gray and grim, this morning, and I feel it would be a comfort to have a piping voice, and broken back, and scare little children. Dont *you* run, Susie dear, for I wont do any harm, and I do love you dearly tho' I do feel so frightful.

Oh my darling one, how long you wander from me, how weary I grow of waiting and looking, and calling for you; sometimes I shut my eyes, and shut my heart towards you, and try hard to forget you because you grieve me so, but you'll never go away, Oh you never will – say, Susie, promise me again, and I will smile faintly – and take up my little cross again of sad – *sad* separation. How vain it seems to *write*, when one knows how to feel – how much more near and dear to sit beside you, talk with you, hear the tones of your voice; so hard to 'deny thyself, and take up thy cross, and follow me' – give me strength, Susie, write me of hope and love, and of hearts that *endured*, and great was their reward of 'Our Father who art in Heaven.' I dont know how I shall bear it, when the gentle spring comes; if she should come and see me and talk to me of you, Oh it would surely kill me! While the frost clings to the windows, and the World is stern and drear; this absence is easier; the *Earth* mourns too, for all her little birds; but when they all come back again, and she sings and is so merry – pray, what will become of me? Susie, forgive me, forget all what I say, get some sweet little scholar to read a gentle hymn, about Bethleem and Mary, and you will sleep on sweetly and have as peaceful dreams, as if I had never written you all these ugly things. Never mind the letter Susie, I wont be angry with you if you dont give me any at all – for I know how busy you are, and how little of that dear strength remains when it is evening, with which to think and write. Only *want* to write me, only sometimes sigh that you are far from me, and that will do, Susie! Dont you think we are good and patient, to let you go so long; and dont we think you're a darling, a real beautiful hero, to toil for people, and teach them, and leave your own dear home? Because we pine and repine, dont think we forget the precious patriot at war in other lands! Never be mournful, Susie – be happy and have cheer, for how many of the long days have gone away since I wrote you – and it is almost noon, and soon the night will come, and then there is one less day of the long pilgrimage. Mattie is very smart, talks of you *much*, my darling; I must leave you now – 'one little hour of Heaven,' thank who did give it me, and will he also grant me one longer and *more* when it shall please his love – bring Susie home, ie! Love always, and ever, and true!

Emily –

EDITH WHARTON (1862–1937)
USA

Currently the subject of a revival in the USA, where two of her works on fashionable American society life in the early twentieth century have been made into major films. Edith Wharton published more than forty volumes in her lifetime: novels, stories, verse, essays, travel books and memoirs. Ethan Frome *(1911) is probably her best-known work, although least typical of her art. Her other novels include* The House of Mirth *(1905) and* The Age of Innocence *(1920), which won a Pulitzer Prize.*

Born Edith Newbold Jones to a wealthy New York family, she was married in 1885 to 'Teddy' Wharton, a Harvard graduate with 'no vocation and no income'. Sexually, the marriage was disastrous. It was not until she was in her late forties, in Paris, in 1908, that Wharton had her first and last sexual awakening, falling deliriously in love with the American journalist William Morton Fullerton. Morton Fullerton was an experienced seducer, and the romance was heady but short-lived. It none the less fuelled a creative outburst in Wharton which yielded, amongst other major works, Ethan Frome*. In 1913 she divorced her husband and made her home permanently in France.*

*She is writing here to W. Morton Fullerton in the early days of their liaison. (See also **Declaration**.)*

To W. Morton Fullerton

Wed Evening
[58 Rue de Varenne
Early March 1908]

Do you want me to lunch with you tomorrow, cuor mio? Getting home just now, I find myself put-off by Rosa, owing to Henri de L.'s illness. – So I can slip off beautifully – if you have time & are free. Please say *frankly*, won't you, if it's not convenient? I should like it to be somewhere at the end of the earth (rive gauche) where there is bad food, & no chance of meeting acquaintances. – If you tell me where, I'll come – or better, meet you at the Louvre at one o'c, in the shadow of Jean Gougon's Diana. – *Let me know early.* If not, then on Friday, same combinazione. –

No, I won't give up, no, I won't believe it's the end, no, I am going to fight for my life – I know it now!

Keep Friday evening if you can.

DECLARATION:
'Well, then let slip the masks'

EDITH WHARTON (1862–1937)
USA

(See also **Invitation**.)

To W. Morton Fullerton

[58 Rue de Varenne
Early March 1908]

Dear, Remember, please, how impatient & anxious I shall be to know the sequel of the Bell letter. . . .

—Do you know what I was thinking last night, when you asked me, & I couldn't tell you? – Only that the way you've spent your emotional life, while I've – bien malgré moi – hoarded mine, is what puts the great gulf between us, & sets us not only on opposite shores, but at hopelessly distant points of our respective shores. . . . Do you see what I mean?

And I'm so afraid that the treasures I long to unpack for you, that have come to me in magic ships from enchanted islands, are only, to you, the old familiar red calico & beads of the clever trader, who has had dealings in every latitude, & knows just what to carry in the hold to please the simple native – I'm so afraid of this, that often & often I stuff my shining treasures back into their box, lest I should see you smiling at them!

Well! And if you do? It's *your* loss, after all! And if you can't come into the room without my feeling all over me a ripple of flame, & if, wherever you touch me, a heart beats under your touch, & if, when you hold me, & I don't speak, it's because all the words in me seem to have become throbbing pulses, & all my thoughts are a great golden blur – why should I be afraid of your smiling at me, when I can turn the beads & calico back into such beauty –?

GILLIAN HANSCOMBE (*b.* 1945)
Australia/England

SUNITI NAMJOSHI (*b.* 1941)
India/England

In addition to many other works, poets Namjoshi and Hanscombe are joint authors of the volume Flesh and Paper *(Jezebel Tapes and Books), from which these poem-letters are taken. Namjoshi and Hanscombe met at a conference in London in 1984, and began a love affair and correspondence between London and Toronto. As for which came first, Hanscombe says: 'The poems came first. . . . The flesh followed predictably.' They now live together in Dorset. (See also* ***Consummation****.)*

To Suniti Namjoshi

Christ how my circumspect heart

Christ how my
circumspect
heart goes
spinning between beats
throat goes
dry as old bark
blood in my
ears goes banging

so
having undone me
                    will you
gather me kindly
lay
hands on my eyelids
flowers in the
cleft of my breasts

you oh you
have
discovered me
unsealed my longing
appointed me mighty

named me

To Gillian Hanscombe

Well, then let slip the masks

Well, then let slip the masks
    and all the notes we have taken,
let them fall to the ground and turn into petals
to make more luxurious our bed, or let them
turn into leaves and blow in the air, let them
make patterns, let them amuse themselves.
The curve of your breast is like the curve
of a wave: look, held, caught, each instant
caught, the wave tipping over and we in our bower,
the two of us sheltered, my hands on your thighs,
your body, your back, my mouth on your mouth
and in the hollows of your jaws and your head
nuzzling my breasts. And the wave above us is
folding over now, folding and laughing. Will you
take to the sea, my darling? Will you let me caress you?
The tips of your feet, your legs, your sex?
Will you let my tongue caress you? Will you
lie in my arms? Will you rest? And if the sun
is too strong, should burn too much, will you
walk with me to where the light is more calm
and be in me where the seas heave and are
serene and heave again and are themselves?

CLARA WIECK (1819–96)
Germany

Clara Wieck was a brilliant pianist, courted by the composer Robert Schumann. Her musical gift helped to popularise Schumann's music, particularly after he permanently injured his right hand, and was unable to play himself. Schumann begged Clara to marry him on many occasions, but her father was against it. Clara's heart was indeed steadfast – as she claims in this letter to Schumann, written just before her eighteenth birthday – and they did eventually marry.

To Robert Schumann

Leipzig, 15 August, 1837

You require but a simple 'Yes'? Such a small word – but such an important one. But should not a heart so full of unutterable love as mine utter this little word with all its might? I do so and my innermost soul whispers always to you.

The sorrows of my heart, the many tears, could I depict them to you – oh no! Perhaps fate will ordain that we see each other soon and then – your intention seems risky to me and yet a loving heart does not take much count of dangers. But once again I say to you 'Yes.' Would God make my eighteenth birthday a day of woe? Oh no! that would be too horrible. Besides I have long felt 'it must be,' nothing in the world shall persuade me to stray from what I think right and I will show my father that the youngest of hearts can also be steadfast in purpose.

Your Clara.

VIRGINIA WOOLF (1882–1941)
England

(See also **Invitation**, **Consummation**, **Desolation** and **Celebration**.)
The following letter, hinting at vulnerability, was a 'declaration' by Woolf's standards, as the recipient, Vita Sackville-West, was quick to recognise.

To Vita Sackville-West

Monk's House
Rodmell
Lewes
Sussex
19 August

My dear Vita,
Have you come back, and have you finished your book – when will you let us have it? Here I am, being a nuisance, with all these questions.

I enjoyed your intimate letter from the Dolomites. It gave me a great deal of pain – which is I've no doubt the first stage of intimacy – no friends, no heart, only an indifferent head. Never mind: I enjoyed your abuse very much. . . .

But I will not go on else I should write you a really intimate letter, and then you would dislike me, more, even more, than you do.

But please let me know about the book.

Berg

MARY WORDSWORTH (1782–1859)
England

'I never see a flower that pleases me, but I wish for you,' wrote the poet William Wordsworth to his wife Mary in 1810, after eight years of marriage. Her letters to him were bought as scrap for £5 by a stamp dealer in Carlisle, and came up for auction at Sotheby's in 1977. The value of the find only then became evident. Mary's ardent words to William and her delicate allusion to the first night they spent together offers a glimpse of their marriage as tender and sensuous, and of Mary herself (hitherto overshadowed by Wordsworth's sister Dorothy) as warm, intelligent and expressive, and an important influence in Wordsworth's life.

To William Wordsworth (extract)

Grasmere Aug. 1st – Wednesday Mor^{g} –

O My William!
it is not in my power to tell thee how I have been affected by this dearest of all letters – it was so unexpected – so new a thing to see the breathing of thy inmost heart upon paper that I was quite overpowered, & now that I sit down to answer thee in the loneliness & depth of that love which unites us & which cannot be felt but by ourselves, I am so agitated & my eyes are so bedimmed that I scarcely know how to proceed – I have brought my paper, after having laid my baby upon thy sacred pillow, into my own, into THY own room – & write from Sara's little Table, retired from the window which looks upon the lasses strewing out the hay to an uncertain Sun. – [. . .]

I look upon thy letter & I marvel how thou hast managed to write it so legibly, for there is not a word in it, that I could have a doubt about. But how is it that I have not received it sooner – It was written on *Sunday* before last – last Sunday *Morning* I rec^{d}. one of Dear Dorothy's written on the *Monday* & another in the evening of the same day, written on the *Thursday*; both *since* that day when my good angel put it into thy thoughts to make me so happy – Dorothy has asked me more than once when she has found me this morning with thy letter in my hand 'what I was crying about' – I told her that I was *so happy* – but she could not comprehend this. Indeed my love it has made me supremely blessed – it has given me a new feeling, for it is the first letter of love that has been exclusively my own – Wonder not then that I have been so affected by it.

Dearest William! I am sorry about thy eye – that it is not well before now, & I am SORRY for what causes in me such pious & exulting gladness – that you cannot fully enjoy your absence from me – indeed William I feel, I *have felt* that you cannot, but it overpowers me to be told it by your own pen *I* was much moved by the lines written with your hand in one of D's letters where you spoke of coming home thinking you 'would be of great use' to me – indeed my love thou wouldst but I did not *want thee* so much *then*, as I do now that our uncomfortableness is passed away – if you had been here, no *doubt* there would have existed in me that underconsciousness that I had my *all in all* about me – *that* feeling which I have never wanted since* the solitary night did not separate us, except in absence; but I had not then that leisure which I ought to have & which is necessary to be actively alive to so rich a possession & to the full enjoyment of it – I *do* William & I shall to the end of my life consider this sacrifice as a dear offering of thy love, I feel it to be such, & I am grateful to thee for it but I trust that it will be the last of the kind that we shall need to make –

*'I slept with' was deleted.

NINON DE L'ENCLOS (1616–1706)
France

The French courtesan Ninon de l'Enclos was so famous for her beauty that – rumour has it – the son she had not seen since birth fell in love with her and shot himself on learning the truth. Others who fell at her feet (or rather, congregated at her salon) included Molière, Fontanelle and La Rochefoucauld. Here she writes to the Marquis de Sévigné, and it becomes obvious that her magnetic power with men was not due only to her famed beauty but also to the fact that Ninon de l'Enclos was a great wit, and a virtuoso in the art of the love letter.

To the Marquis de Sévigné

Shall I tell you what renders love dangerous? It is the sublime idea which one often appears to have about it. But in exact truth, Love, taken as a passion, is only a blind instinct which one must know how to value correctly; an *appetite* which determines you for one object rather than for another, without being able to give any reason for one's preference; considered as a link of friendship, when reason presides over it, it is not a passion, it is no longer love, it is an affectionate esteem, in truth, but peaceful, incapable of leading you out of bounds; when, however, you walk in the traces of our ancient heroes of romance, you go in for the grand sentiments, you will see that this pretended heroism only makes of love a deplorable and often disastrous folly. It is a true fanaticism; but if you strip it of all those virtues of hearsay, it will soon minister to your happiness and to your pleasures. Believe me, that if it were reason or enthusiasm which governed affairs of the heart, love would become either insipid or a delirium. The only way to avoid these two extremes is to follow the path I indicate to you. You have need of being amused and you will only find what you require for that amongst the women I speak of. Your heart needs occupation; they are made to captivate it. . . .

Honesty in love, marquis! How can you think of that! Ah, you are a good man gone wrong. I shall take great care not to show your letter; you would be dishonoured. You could not, you say, take on yourself to employ the manoeuvre which I have counselled you. Your frankness, your grandiose sentiments would have made your fortune in the old days. Then one used to treat love as a matter of honour; but today, when the corruption of the century has changed everything, Love is no more than a play of whim and vanity. . . . How many occasions do you not find where a lover gains as much by dissimulating the excess of his passion, as he would in others, by displaying greater passion than he feels?

MARY MEIGS (*b.* 1917)
Canada

An 'extraordinary love adventure' between Mary Meigs and a slightly younger woman, whom she identifies only as 'R', began in 1992, with a love letter. 'R', then sixty-eight, wrote enthusiastically to Meigs from Australia, having seen her in the film The Company of Strangers *and having also read Meigs's first book,* Lily Briscoe: A Self-Portrait, *while on a visit to Canada. The correspondence between them blossomed into an intense relationship, with a series of extended visits between Sydney and Quebec. Meigs is currently working on a book,* The Time Being, *which recounts their remarkable love story. Here she gives her response to a first photograph of 'R'.*

To 'R' (extracts)

August 2, 1992: You evidently have a dimple just above the corner of your mouth, stage right which is really left? when you smile at me, a little light on your cheek and you're so radiantly beautiful! I wanted to send you a drawing to show the parts of my right-hand face that are still hyper-sensitive, perhaps always will be? So if I jump, in one of our long and lovely kissing seances you won't think it's your fault, my consummately careful darling. I wish we were in the middle of one right now, silently moving over each other's faces with resting-places, passionate ones, to linger at and in. I've lost my power over words and spent (after wandering around looking for raspberries and being bitten by bugs) a good part of the afternoon asleep on the sofa while the last Haydn trios were playing with slow movements written just for us. I've been thinking of *your* power over words, rather like a ballet mistress, and they are beautifully trained to follow your choreography so gracefully that they don't seem to have worked at it. I'm looking at your August 7th letter and your stern theory (based on my warnings, of course) of my tiny percentage of 'sex/physical and all that,' total control indeed. Our total control seems to have slipped a bit, doesn't it, and I wonder if I, for one, ever had it or was just basing my conception of it on past experience, for I had to learn what a mere photo of you can do to my corporeal soul. As for *your* soul, my love, when did the 'demonstrative R' go too far? And which of us is ahead of the other?

October 7, 1992: What makes you think I like 'boyish' bodies, what gave you that idea? Would that mine could be called 'boyish' when, in fact, it's *under*-endowed in most departments; some would call me flat-chested. About what you call your over-endowment I laughed (your handwriting becomes mildly indecipherable at this point, but I managed to decipher it and laughed even harder), also at your delusion that this 'may reduce the arousal-quotient,' since you seem to be boyish and 'over-endowed' in all the right places. Also to have an inexhaustible power to arouse, judging by the long list of aroused women in your past. . . . And your map of the apt. is great and enables me to prowl around it at all hours of the day and night, occasionally bumping into you and clasping you in a frenetic embrace.

COLETTE (1873–1954)
France

Sidonie Gabrielle Colette's early works, novels which launched the character of the saucy schoolgirl Claudine, were an instant hit with the French public. They were written under the aegis of Colette's first husband, Willy, and have been the subject of some dispute. She went on to write over seventy texts between 1900 and 1949, earning herself enduring celebrity and eminence as an author.

Her love life was unconventional. A very public liaison with the countess known as 'Missy' ended her first marriage. She married again, this time to a powerful publisher, and produced such classics as Chéri *and* The Ripening Seed. *She finally settled down with the gentle Maurice Goudeket, sixteen years her junior, and it is this new lover whom she is here describing to her 'greatest friend', Marguerite Moreno. (See also* ***Celebration****.)*

To Marguerite Moreno (extracts)

June 11, 1925

What am I doing? Heavens, I'm spinning. And I use this verb as a planet would. Yes, I'm spinning. I've seen roses, honeysuckle, forty degrees Centigrade of dazzling heat, moonlight, ancient wisteria enlacing the door of my old home in Saint-Sauveur. I've seen the night over Fontainebleau. And as I said, I'm spinning. Beside me there is a dark boy at the wheel. I'm on my way back to Paris, but shall I stay there? The dark boy beside me is still at the wheel, and how strange everything is! And how good I am, and how amazed I am, and what wise improvidence in my behavior! Oh yes, I'm spinning!

As you can see, you must not worry about me. From time to time I am uneasy about myself, and I give a start, prick up my ears, and cry out, 'But what are you doing?' and then I refuse to think any more about it. . . .

Just now, on the telephone, an enlightened Chiwawa, enlightened by the dark, dark, dark boy, sang my praises. The era of frankness is back and the cards are on the table. But, my Marguerite, how strange it all is! . . . I have the fleeting confidence of people who fall out of a clock tower and for a moment sail through the air in a comfortable fairy-world, feeling no pain anywhere. . . .

Beauvallon, August 5, 1925

. . . the sparrow owls are hooting under the full moon and I sleep on the terrace. . . . The sea and the sand have become my native elements. So is love. Am I not an abominable creature? (I need you to assure me otherwise.) Because it's three o'clock in the afternoon, my charming companion is sleeping, but I don't need a siesta, I sleep so well at night. One always feels a little guilty writing next to someone who is asleep, even when it is only to acknowledge that he is charming and that one loves him. Tell me, wasn't it last winter that you warned me that *during a voyage* I would meet a man 'who would change my life'?

Translated by R. Phelps

NELL GWYN (1650–87)
England

Legendary mistress of – amongst others – King Charles II. Here Nell Gwyn is writing to Lawrence Hyde, who became Earl of Rochester.

To Lawrence Hyde (extract)

(*circa* 1678)

Pray Deare Mr Hide forgive me for not writeing to you before now for the reasone is I have bin sick thre months and sinse I recovered I have had nothing to intertaine you withall nor have nothing now worth writing but that I can holde no longer to let you know I never have ben in any companie wethout drinking your health for I love you with all my soule.

KWEI-LI (19th Century)
China

Kwei-li was a well-educated young woman of the upper classes who married a high-ranking Chinese official. He became Governor of Kiang Su, a job which frequently took him away on business. The love letters of Kwei-li, published as The Love Letters of a Chinese Lady, *were written from her palatial mountainside home just outside the city of Su-Chau. She was tutored by the famous Chinese poet Ling Wing-pu. (See also* ***Desolation****.)*

To a new husband

Dost thou remember when first thou raised my veil and looked long into my eyes? I was thinking, 'Will he find me beautiful?' and in fear I could look but for a moment, then my eyes fell and I would not raise them to thine again. But in that moment I saw that thou wert tall and beautiful, that thine eyes were truly almond, that thy skin was clear and thy teeth like pearls. I was secretly glad within my heart, because I have known of brides who, when they saw their husbands for the first time, wished to scream in terror, as they were old or ugly. I thought to myself that I could be happy with this tall, strong young man if I found favour in his sight, and I said a little prayer to Kwan-yin. Because she has answered that prayer, each day I place a candle at her feet to show my gratitude.

Translated by Elizabeth Cooper

ADULATION:
'There is only you'

KATHERINE MANSFIELD (1888–1923)
New Zealand

Katherine Mansfield is New Zealand's most famous writer; her perfection of the short story transformed the genre for ever. As a young woman she came to London originally to attend Queen's College. After a brief visit in 1906, she never returned to New Zealand.

In London she led a 'bohemian' lifestyle, marrying George Bowden and leaving him the following day, touring with a musical company. She met John Middleton Murry while he was the editor of Rhythm, *a journal to which she submitted stories, and they lived together until their marriage in 1918. The following letters were written to John Middleton Murry during the couple's many separations, while Mansfield was in France, suffering from tuberculosis.*

To John Middleton Murry

1st Morning

13 Quai aux Fleurs, Paris
[Friday, 19th March 1915]

My dearest darling,
I have just had déjeuner – a large bowl of hot milk and a small rather inferior orange – but still not dressed or washed or at all a nice girl, I want to write to you. The sun is very warm today and lazy – the kind of sun that loves to make patterns out of shadows and puts freckles on sleeping babies – a pleasant creature.

Bogey, I had a vile and loathsome journey. We trailed out of London in a fog that thickened all the way. A hideous little Frenchwoman in a mackintosh with a little girl in a dirty face and a sailor suit filled and overflowed my carriage. The child combed its hair with a lump of brown bread, spat apple in our faces – made the Ultimate impossible noises – ugh! how vile! Only one thing rather struck me. It pointed out of the window and peeped its eternal 'Qu'est-ce?' 'C'est de la *terre*, ma petite,' said the mother, indifferent as a cabbage. Folkestone looked like a picture painted on a coffin lid and Boulogne like one painted on a sardine tin. Between them rocked an oily sea. I stayed on deck and felt nothing when the destroyer signalled our ship. We were 2 hours late arriving and then the train to Paris did not even trot once – sauntered – meandered. Happily an old Scotchman, one time captain of the 'California', that big ship that went down in the fog off Tory Island, sat opposite to me and we 'got chatting'. He was a Scotchman with a pretty, soft accent;

when he laughed he put his hand over his eyes and his face never changed – only his belly shook. But he was 'extremely nice' – quite as good as 1s. Worth of Conrad. At Amiens he found a tea-wagon and bought ham and fresh rolls and oranges and wine and would not be paid, so I ate hearty. Paris looked exactly like anywhere else – it smelled faintly of lavatories. The trees appeared to have shed their buds. So I took a room (the same room) and piled up coats and shawls on my bed to 'sleep and forget'. It was all merely dull beyond words and stupid and meaningless.

But today the sun is out: I must dress and follow him. Bless you my dearest dear. I love you *utterly* – *utterly* – beyond words – and I will not be sad. I will not take our staying in our own rooms for a little as anything serious. How are you? What are you doing?

Address my letters to the post until I give you another address.

This is a silly old letter – like eating ashes with a fish-fork – but it is not meant to be. I rather wanted to tell you the truth. I read last night in the *Figaro* that the 16th Section (Carco's) are to be sent to TURKEY Alas, the day!

Jaggle, Bogey, love – tell me about you, your book, your rooms – everything.

Your Tig

[28th March 1915]

Jack, I shan't hide what I feel today. I woke up with you in my breast and on my lips. Jack, I love you terribly today. The whole world is gone. There is only you. I walk about, dress, eat, write – but all the time I am *breathing* you. Time and again I have been on the point of telegraphing you that I am coming home as soon as Kay sends my money. It is still possible that I shall.

Jack, Jack, I want to come back,
And to hear the little ducks go
Quack! Quack! Quack!

Life is too short for our love even though we stayed together every moment of all the years. I cannot think of you – our life – our darling life – you, my treasure – everything about you.

No, no, no. Take me quickly into your arms. Tig is a tired girl and she is crying. I want you, I want you. Without you life is nothing.

Your woman Tig

MARINA TSVETAYEVA (1892–1941)
Russia

Marina Tsvetayeva is now recognised as one of the greatest Russian poets of the twentieth century. She was born in Moscow and raised in an artistic family. In 1914, married and with a daughter, she became intimately involved with the poet Sofia Parnok. The affair produced the cycle of poems Girlfriend. *Tsvetayeva's most famous work is probably the powerful narrative poem* The Poem of the End, *written in 1924.*

In the summer of 1926 Tsvetayeva began an astonishing correspondence with two other writers with formidable reputations: the German writer Rainer Maria Rilke and fellow Russian Boris Pasternak. Pasternak was her close friend, introducing her by letter to his idol, Rilke.

Here Tsvetayeva is addressing Rilke, after his death. She enclosed the letter, written in German, with one to Pasternak, on hearing of Rilke's death from leukaemia at the end of 1926.

To Rilke

Bellevue
December 31, 1926. 10 p.m.

The year ended in your death? The end? The beginning! You yourself are the New Year. (Beloved, I know you are reading this before I write it.) I am crying, Rainer, you are streaming from my eyes!

Dear one, now that you are dead there is no death (or no life!). What can I say? That little town in Savoy – when? where? Rainer, what about that 'nest' to keep our dreams in? Now Russian is an open book to you, so you know that the Russian word for 'nest' is *gnezdo.* And you know so many other things.

I don't want to reread your letter or I will want to join you – there – and I dare not wish for such a thing. You know what such a wish implies.

Rainer, I am always conscious of your presence at my shoulder.

Did you ever think of me? Yes, of course you did.

Tomorrow is New Year's Day, Rainer. 1927. Seven is your favorite number. You were born in 1875 (newspaper date?). Fifty-one years old?

How disconsolate I am!

Don't dare to grieve! At midnight tonight I will drink with you (you know how I clink glasses – ever so lightly!).

Beloved, come to me often in my dreams. No, not that. Live in my dreams. Now you have a right to wish and to fulfill your wishes.

You and I never believed in our meeting here on earth, any more than we believed in life on this earth, isn't that so? You have gone before me (and that is better!), and to receive me well you have taken not a room, not a house, but a whole landscape. I kiss you . . . on the lips? on the temple? on the forehead? Of course on the lips, for real, as if alive.

Beloved, love me more and differently from others. Don't be angry with me. You must grow accustomed to me, to such a one as I am. What else?

No, you are not yet far away and high above, you are right here, with your head on my shoulder. You will never be far away: never inaccessibly high.

You are my darling grown-up boy.

Rainer, write to me! (A foolish request?)

Happy New Year and may you enjoy the heavenly landscape!

Marina

Rainer, you are still on this earth; twenty-four hours have not yet passed.

HESTER PIOZZI (1741–1821)
England

As Hester Thrale she was the well-known friend of Samuel Johnson. Sadly, for the purposes of this book, when she married Gabriele Piozzi in 1784 Johnson 'drove the memory of Mrs Thrale from his mind, burning every letter of hers on which he could lay a hand*'.*

On Piozzi's death, she returned to Bath. There she became infatuated with a handsome young actor, William Augustus Conway. Her letters to him begin in 1819, when she was seventy-three and the young man twenty-six. HLP is her nickname for herself.

To William Augustus Conway (extract)

Feb. 3, 1820

'Tis not a year and quarter since dear Conway, accepting of my portrait sent to Birmingham, said to the bringer – 'oh if *your lady* but retains her friendship; oh if I can but keep *her* patronage – I care not for the rest.' . . . And now, when that friendship follows you through sickness and through sorrow, now that her patronage is daily rising in importance – upon a lock of hair given . . . or refused by une petite traitresse – hangs all the happiness of my once high-spirited and high-blooded friend. Let it not be so. Exalt Thy Love-Dejected Heart, and rise superior to such narrow minds. Do not however fancy she will be ever punished in the way you mention; no, no. She'll wither on the thorny stem, dropping the faded and ungathered leaves – a China rose, of no good scent or flavour – false in apparent sweetness, deceitful when depended on. Unlike the flower produced in colder climates, which is sought for in old age, preserved even after death, a lasting and an elegant perfume – a medicine, too, for those whose shattered nerves require astringent remedies.

Let me request of you . . . to love yourself, . . . and to reflect on the necessity of not dwelling on any particular subject too long or too intensely. . . .

This is preaching, but remember how the sermon is written at three, four, and five o'clock by an octogenarian pen, a heart twenty-six years old, and as H.L.P. feels it to be all your own.

ALICE MAUDE BROWNE (19th Century)
Britain

After the death of her beloved maiden aunt, Mary Salter Browne, in 1906, Alice Maude painstakingly put together a book of letters, photographs, pictures and poems. She bound and printed it herself, dedicated it to her aunt, and distributed it amongst close family and friends. It was called You and I Together Love.

To Mary Salter Browne (extract)

Hôtel d'Angleterre, Venice
May 24, 1907

My own darling, – It has been such a great sorrow and deprivation to me not to have you to write to as I have always done so fully and so regularly whenever hitherto we have been separated, even for a day or so. And there will never be anyone to fill your place in my heart – no one to whom I can write with such freedom of all the wonderful things I have seen, and am still seeing, since you were called to take the long journey from which there is no return; no one I am convinced, to whom my letters can ever be so welcome as they always were to you.

And how welcome were yours to me! For whenever we were parted you would write me fully of your doings, and the sights you were seeing, so that I could picture your surroundings and rejoice with you in the beauties you were always so quick to discover and so graphically describe.

Ah, if only you could tell me what your dear eyes now look upon! If only I might speak to you of the things I am seeing!

And this morning as I lay awake in this wonderful city of Venice, my mind full of its lovelinesses, overcharged too with the longing to disclose them to you, I said to myself, 'Why should you not write to your Dearest?'

ANNE SEXTON (1928–74)
USA

Born in Massachusetts to upper-middle-class parents, Sexton was from the first given to dramatic gestures, and at the age of nineteen she eloped to Boston. She trained and worked as a model, and began writing poetry while attending adult education workshops. At one time she attended the workshops of Robert Lowell, with fellow poet Sylvia Plath. Her best-known poetry collections are To Bedlam and Part Way Back *(1960),* All my Pretty Ones *(1962) and* Live or Die *(1966).*

Sexton struggled for most of her life with depressions and madness. After a failed suicide attempt in 1956, at the age of twenty-eight, she began psychotherapy sessions which continued until her death from suicide in 1974.

Here Sexton has just been introduced, by the writer Tillie Olsen (whom she admired fervently), to Anne Clarke, a psychiatrist from California. They immediately formed a strong friendship which survived over the years via the post, in spite of Sexton's repeated attempts to cast her friend in the role of her therapist, something Clarke fought to resist. *(See also* ***Celebration****.)*

To Anne Clarke (extract)

[40 Clearwater Road]
jan what the hell is the
date . . . I guess it's prob the 21st or
something . . . no 22nd . . .
1964

Sweet Anne,
I love you. Do you know how I look for the mail and it is your letter that I hunt for, that I spring from the desk for when I hear the mailman slip his letters thru the lock. Yep! It's your envelope I hunt for. Yep! It's your voice. Your cadence!

Okay? [. . .]

Anne, the thing that really is bugging me, putting me, mouth at the wall (I *mean* wall) is that Dr Martin is leaving . . . Christ. I can't. I *mean* I can't. That's all. I just can't. Christ's sake! How can I explain . . . it would take too many pages . . . hours . . . get the picture, Anne . . . eight years of therapy. . . . At start me nothing . . . *really* nothing . . . for two years me still nothing . . . and then I start to be something and then my mother dies, and then father . . . a large storm . . . then recovery and that slow and trying to both Martin and me . . . I mean 'hell' not just 'trying' (and, for him too) . . . (I'm a very difficult, acting out patient) . . . and I'd come quite far , , , , but now . . . now . . . if he goes next Sept. and he thinks he will . . . I have had it. I can't make it (the intense trust, *the* transference all over AGAIN) . . . Anne! Please! Help me! Don't be my doctor . . . but for God's sake be my friend who is also a doctor. I could use that. I mean, I not only could use it . . . but it might be essential for me for a time . . . I HAVE GOT TO HAVE SOMEONE. (Am I too dramatic . . . after all, I know I'm not dying . . . not really . . . but it [is] so close . . . as you said, just as you said. When you die you are really alone. I mean no one is going along with you and you'd like to do it without losing control, to maintain a little pride, a little respect . . .) . . . Anne, I feel so alone. I think, between you and me, that I'm half so well and half so sick . . . and I don't want the sick to win . . . to lose all control . . . but . . .

but . . .

alone . . .

ABIGAIL SMITH (1744–?)
USA

Abigail Smith was born in Weymouth, Massachusetts, the daughter of a Congregational minister. In 1764 she married John Adams, who was to become the second President of the United States. As Abigail Adams she was an influential woman at the time of the American Revolution. Here she is writing to John Adams, before her marriage.

To John Adams (extract)

Friday morning, April 20th (1764)

What does it signify? Why may I not visit you days as well as nights? I no sooner close my eyes, than some invisible being, swift as the Alborack of Mahomet, bears me to you – I see you, but cannot make myself visible to you. That tortures me, but it is still worse when I do not come, for I am then haunted by half a dozen ugly sprites. One will catch me and leap into the sea; another will carry me up a precipice like that which Edgar describes in Lear, then toss me down, and, were I not then light as the gossamer, I should shiver into atoms; another will be pouring down my throat stuff worse than the witches' broth in Macbeth. Where I shall be carried next I know not, but I would rather have the smallpox by inoculation half a dozen times than be sprited about as I am. What say you? Can you give me any encouragement to come? By the time you receive this I hope from experience you will be able to say that the distemper is but a trifle. Think you I would not endure a trifle for the pleasure of seeing you? Yes, were it ten times that trifle, I would. But my own inclinations must not be followed, – to duty I sacrifice them. Yet, O my mamma, forgive me if I say, you have forgot or never knew – but hush, and do you excuse me that something I promised you, since it was a speech more undutiful than that which I just now stopped myself in. For the present, goodbye.

IPPOLITA TORELLI (16th Century)
Italy

Wife of Baldassare Castiglione.

To her husband Baldassare Castiglione (extract)

1516

My Lord, you alone are impressed upon my memory and continually I seem to see you before me. Gossiping tongues full of malice have not been of such strength that my own tongue has not been able to silence them, letting them understand that I do not believe there is a happier woman than I am in the whole world. This, my sweet husband, is still the truth, and I have been unable to effect a worse revenge on them than that; so that not knowing how to speak further ill of Your Lordship, they have turned against me saying that I am a piece of meat with two eyes. It now remains for you, my Lord, to defend me, to be my shield. I am happy to wait until I come to Mantua. I thank you, my Lord, for the ruff. Nothing could please me more than it does, nothing could be more dear to me than its lovely form. I do not wish once again, my Lord, to remind you to keep me in your memory. I am hoping to see you soon, and since for the sweetness of writing I feel myself bereft of the little sense that Your Lordship has left me, I will come to an end, begging you to send my best wishes to all our relatives there. And I embrace and kiss Your Lordship. The illustrious Ladies Bianca and Catelina, and Isabetta and Cecilia and all the other women of the house send Your Lordship their wishes.

That wife who without Your Lordship would be unable to write

Translated by Jamie McKendrick

JULIE-JEANNE-ELÉONORE DE L'ESPINASSE (1732–76)
France

The letters of Julie de l'Espinasse to her lover, the Comte de Guibert, are considered a classic in French literature. A brilliant wit, de l'Espinasse attracted many notable Frenchmen to her salon, although Marjorie Bowen, in her book Some Famous Love Letters, *still manages to describe her as 'socially non-existent, sickly, pock-marked' and 'middle-aged'. (She was thirty-five.)*

De l'Espinasse's overwhelming passion for the Comte, summed up in her words 'I suffer, I love you, and I await you', is said to have killed her.

To the Comte de Guibert

November 13th, 1774

Ah, my friend, you hurt me, and a great curse for you and for me is the feeling which animates me. You were right in saying that you did not need to be loved as I know how to love; no, that is not your measure; you are so perfectly lovable, that you must be or become the first object (of desire) of all these charming ladies, who stick upon their heads all they had in it, and who are so lovable that they love themselves by preference above everything. You will give pleasure, you will satisfy the vanity of nearly all women. By what fatality have you held me to life, and you make me die of anxiety and of pain? My friend, I do not complain; but it distresses me that you pay no heed to my repose; this thought chills and tears my heart alternately. How can one have an instant's tranquillity with a man whose head is as defective as his coach, who counts for nothing the dangers, who never foresees anything, who is incapable of taking care, of exactitude, to whom it never happens to do what he has projected; in a word, a man whom everything attracts, and whom nothing can stay nor give stability. . . . Good night. My door has not been opened once today, but what my heart palpitated. There were moments when I feared to hear your voice, and then I was disconsolate that it was not your voice. So many contradictions, so many contrary movements are true, and can be explained in three words: *I love you.*

EMPRESS ALEXANDRA (1872–1918)
Russia

As Princess Alexandra she was the granddaughter of Queen Victoria, and grew up in Kensington Palace before marrying the Tsar of Russia, Nicholas II, when she was nineteen. They were a doting couple, addressing each other in the Russian palace with the English pet names Hubby and Wifey.

As Tsarina, Alexandra fell under the spell of the peasant Rasputin, who was magically able to cure her son of haemophilia. 'Our Friend' Rasputin soon had the entire palace in his thrall, with disastrous consequences for the Tsar.

It was once presumed that Alexandra was killed by the Bolsheviks with the rest of her family in 1918, but recently there have been controversial suggestions that the Tsar and Tsarina may have fled Russia and escaped execution.

Here she is writing to her husband.

To Tsar Nicholas II (extract)

Lovy dear, my telegrams can't be very warm, as they go through so many military hands – but you will read all my love & longing between the lines. Sweety, if in any way you do not feel quite the thing, you will be sure to call Feodorov, won't you – & have an eye on Fredericks.

My very most earnest prayers will follow you by day and night. I commend you into our Lord's safe keeping – may He guard, guide & lead you & bring you safe & sound back again.

I bless you & love you, as man has rarely been loved before – & kiss every dearly beloved place & press you tenderly to my own heart.

For ever yr. very own old

Wify

The Image will lie this night under my cushion before I give it to you with my fervent blessing.

EDITH THOMPSON (1888–1923)
England

The trial of Edith Thompson – accused of conspiracy to murder her husband, Percy, along with her young lover Frederick Bywaters – caused a sensation in 1922. Although it was clear that Thompson had not assisted in the murder, and had even gone to get help after Freddy had leapt at Percy in the street and stabbed him, she was convicted largely as a result of her love letters to Freddy. These showed that she wished *her husband dead, had perhaps plotted to poison him, and was guilty of adultery with a man nineteen years her junior. For this she was executed, along with Freddy, in 1923.*

Thompson calls herself 'Peidi'.

To Frederick Bywaters

Dec. 6, 1921

Darlingest boy I know,

I saw in the paper yesterday you touched Aden on the 28th, I suppose tomorrow or Sunday you will arrive in Bombay & I believe Bill left today, perhaps you will just manage to see him tho'.

I am feeling very blue today darlint, you havn't talked to me for a fortnight, and I am feeling worried, oh I don't know how I'm feeling really, it seems like a very large pain that comes from that ceaseless longing for you, words are expressionless – darlint, the greatness, the bigness of the love I have, makes me fear that it is too good to last, it will never die, darlint don't think, but I fear – how can I explain – that it will never mature, that we, you & I will never reap our reward, in fact, I just feel today darlint, that our love will all be in vain.

He talked to me again last night a lot, darlint I don't remember much about it, except that he asked me if I was any happier. I just said I suppose as happy as I shall ever be, & then he frightened me by saying – oh I don't think I'll tell you.

I left off there, darlint – thought – thought for 1/2 an hour & I will tell you now. He said he began to think that both of us would be happier if we had a baby, I said 'No, a thousand times No' & he began to question me, and talk to me & plead with me, oh darlint, its all so hard to bear, come home to me – come home quickly and help me, its so much worse this time. He hasn't worried me any more, except that once I told you about, darlint, do you understand what

I mean? but things seem worse for all that. You know I always sleep to the wall, darlint, well I still do but he puts his arm round me and oh its horrid. I suppose I'm silly to take any notice, I never used to – before I knew you – I just used to accept the inevitable, but you know darlint, I either feel things very intensely or I am quite indifferent just cold – frozen.

But to write all this is very selfish of me, it will make you feel very miserable – you can't do anything to help me – at least not yet, so I'll stop. [. . .]

. . . What do you think he is going to learn dancing – to take me out to some nice ones, won't it be fun – as the song says 'Aint we got fun,' while you are away. About myself, darlint, its still the same & I've not done anything yet – I don't think I shall until next month, unless you tell me otherwise, after you get this letter, or the one I wrote previously.

Darlint I got a letter, or rather 2 in 1 envelope on Saturday morning. You say that you can't write but you will try from Port Said. Is this correct? The envelope of these is stamped Port Said. No, you're quite right darlint, when you say you cant talk to me, you can't, these letters are only writing, they are not talking, not the real talking I was looking forward to.

Why is it? darlint, what is the matter? you do still feel the same, don't you? Oh say Yes, I feel so sad & miserable about it. I seem to be able to talk to you always & for ever, but you, I don't know, you don't seem the same as when you were away before, you did talk to me a lot that trip, but this time you don't seem to at all. Why is it darlint? You do still feel the same don't you? Am I horrid to expect so much, tell me if I am but darlint I feel that I could give all, everything & I can't read between the lines of your letters this time that you even want to accept that all.

One part that did amuse me was over the argument. That expression 'I do love 'em, etc.' made me think of old times, you remember the Shanklin times, when neither of us had any cares, or worries, personal ones I mean, altho' we hadn't learned to know ourselves or each other, which were the best times darlint? now or then, just tell me, I shant mind. That was a funny dream you had, wasn't it? I wonder what it means or if it means anything. Why do you tell me not to get excited darlint, do you think I would. I don't think I should darlint, over that, you & I have too much at stake, to take too many risks. But I don't think there is any risk, darlint, it doesn't seem so at any rate. But I feel that I could dare anything, and bear everything for you, darlint.

That's all now, darlint, I've got such a great lump come in my throat & I'll have to swallow it somehow. Peidi does want you now.

Feb. 15, 1922

I was so pleased to get your letter, darlint, it came on Friday midday. Miss Prior took it in & examined the seal – all the time she was bringing it down the stairs. I was looking at her Darlint, you say I cant know how you feel, when you failed cant I darlint? Don't I know didn't I fail once? I do know darlint, its heartbreaking to think all the schemeing – all the efforts are in vain. But we'll be patient darlint the time will come we're going to make it just you & I our united efforts darlint.

EMILY DICKINSON (1830–86)
USA

(See also **Invitation, Consummation** and **Celebration**.)

To Susan Gilbert (Dickinson)

5 April 1852

Will you be kind to me, Susie? I am naughty and cross, this morning, and nobody loves me here; nor would *you* love me, if you should see me frown, and hear how loud the door bangs whenever I go through; and yet it is'nt anger – I dont believe it is, for when nobody sees, I brush away big tears with the corner of my apron, and then go working on – bitter tears, Susie – so hot that they burn my cheeks, and almost schorch my eyeballs, but *you* have wept much and you know they are less of anger than *sorrow*.

And I do love to run fast – and hide away from them all; here in dear Susie's bosom, I know is love and rest, and I never would go away, did not the big world call me, and beat me for not working.

Little *Emerald Mack* is washing, I can hear the warm suds, splash. I just gave her my pocket handkerchief – so I cannot cry any more. And Vinnie sweeps – sweeps, upon the chamber stairs; and Mother is hurrying round with her hair in a silk pocket handkerchief, on account of dust. Oh Susie, it is dismal, sad and drear eno' – and the sun dont shine, and the clouds look cold and gray, and the wind dont blow, but it *pipes* the shrillest roundelay, and the birds dont sing, but twitter – and there's nobody to smile! Do I paint it *natural* – Susie, so you think how it looks? Yet dont you care – for it wont last so always, and we love you just as well – and think of you, as dearly, as if it were not so. Your precious letter, Susie, it sits here now, and smiles so kindly at me, and gives me such sweet thoughts of the dear writer. When you come home, darling, I shant have your letters, shall I, but I shall have *yourself*, which is more – Oh more, and better, than I can even think! I sit here with my little whip, cracking the time away, till not an hour is left of it – then you are here! And *Joy* is here – joy now and forevermore!

BETTINA BRENTANO (1785–1859)
Germany

Bettina Brentano was a woman of letters and a poet. Her infatuation with Prince Hermann von Puckler-Muskau (a famous landscape gardener) was unrequited. She had suffered a similar crush on Goethe when she was nineteen, and written him many similar letters. The following are addressed to the Prince.

To Prince Hermann von Puckler-Muskau

1833

I ask you most earnestly and humbly to return my letters. I shall not see you again, why should the only thing that causes you to regard me with antipathy remain in your hands?

You told me yesterday you did not know what passages [in a book] I had intended for you. Truly, none that was capable of misinterpretation. The friendly inclination which you show to a child coupled with the deep trust which through inviolable fidelity I had wished to win, were a necessity for me in such circumstances.

I have not made this journey to see you; I am not indiscreet, according to your letter I thought you far away. My sole inclination was to enjoy the park, which you call your heart, in silence and through its beautiful charm afford myself a spiritual stimulus in my work. I wanted just to live for myself but I admit that I hoped to give you pleasure thereby.

As I heard that you were here, I had already planned my departure. You invited me to come under your roof but it has turned out other than to your satisfaction nor have I derived much pleasure myself yet I am ready to take all the blame except in this matter, in which you impute it to me.

Whether we communicate directly in future or not, I hope the sincerity of my whole attitude and feelings up to now will never be impugned. My pride is so great that it is invulnerable, no disparaging opinion of me can discourage me. But I willingly admit that it will always be an honour for me to have felt so much at my ease within the bounds of intimacy, in which you called me with such good will.

The messenger will wait to know whether it is your pleasure to return my letters.

Loving and appreciating to the full all that which has by its beauty kept me in true allegiance to you,

I remain,

Your devoted Bettine

1833

Yesterday at midday your gamekeeper came to me and brought in an unsealed, unaddressed and inadequately closed packet, my letters. I had a foreboding that I should be deeply hurt by them. I have read them through tonight and reading them has made me suffer, which you will in all probability not suspect. I am accustomed to draw the waters towards myself. Throughout the whole night I have fought down my claims on you and yet how this love astonishes and pleases me. Ah, Puckler, what a treasure in these buoyant veiled pages hast thou thrown at my feet, just like a dead tree its leaves. And what a thank-offering to your genius that it has given you all this through my agency.

When I estimate the impression these letters have made on me and take your own behaviour into consideration, I see that they are totally indifferent to you, as your manner of returning them testifies and as the unsympathetic, indifferent and heartless-and-soulless way in which you thus belittle the offering I have laid at your feet, amply shows. I was prepared for it, I have no claims on you.

I have willingly taken to heart all the bitter lessons you have taught me. I am now versed in renunciation. In these days you have scourged my soul and I have not even flinched. You have not seen from my laughing features what I felt.

TEMPTATION AND FRUSTRATION: *'I tremble for what we are doing'*

CHARLOTTE BRONTË (1816–55)
England

Author of Jane Eyre *(1847), which was immediately successful; also of* Shirley *(1849),* Villette *(1853) and* The Professor *(1857), published after her death. Along with her famous sisters, Anne and Emily, she also published a book of poetry.*

In 1854, after the death of her brother Branwell, and of Anne and Emily, Charlotte married. She died a year later, while she was pregnant. In the following letters she addresses Ellen Nussey, a dear friend from her schooldays, with whom she formed the most significant relationship of her life.

To Ellen Nussey (extracts)

June 1837

Don't desert me, don't be horrified at me. You know what I am. I wish I could see you, my darling; I have lavished the warmest affections of a very hot tenacious heart upon you – if you grow cold it is over. Love to your mother and sisters.

October 17 1841

Dear Nell,
It is a cruel thing of you to be always upbraiding me when I am a trifle remiss or so in writing a letter. I see I can't make you comprehend that I have not quite as much time on my hands as Miss H. of S. Lane, or Mrs Mills. I never neglect you on purpose. I could not *do* it you little teazing, faithless wretch.

July 14 1841

My Dear Ellen,
We waited long and anxiously for you on the Thursday that you promised to come. I quite wearied my eyes with watching from the window, eye glass in hand, and sometimes spectacles on my nose. . . . But a hundred things I had to say to you will now be forgotten, and never said.

MARIETTA MACHIAVELLI
(Early 16th Century)
Italy

Wife of Niccolò Machiavelli.

To Niccolò Machiavelli

In God's Name
24 December, 1503

My dearest Niccolò,
You scoff at me, but you're wrong to do so as I would be more cheerful if you were here. You well know how happy I am when you're not away down there. And much more so now you've told me that the plague is much in evidence there. So you can guess how calm I feel, finding rest neither day nor night. This is the joy I've had of the baby. But I beg you to send me letters a little more often than you do, as I've received no more than three. You shouldn't marvel that I haven't written. I have been unable to because of the fever I've had until now. I'm not angry. For the moment the baby is well. He looks like you: white as snow, but his head seems to be of black velvet. And he's hairy like you. In that he resembles you, he seems beautiful to me. And from the look of things you'd think he'd already been a year in this world, and had opened his eyes even before he was born, creating a great stir in the whole house. But the little girl is feeling ill. Keep your return in mind. Nothing else. God be with you, and watch over you. I'm sending a doublet and two shirts and two handkerchiefs and a towel, because these things can still be had here,

Your Marietta, in Florence.

Translated by Jamie McKendrick

SIMONE DE BEAUVOIR (1908–86)
France

Simone de Beauvoir, one of the major feminist writers of the twentieth century, met philosopher Jean-Paul Sartre while she was a student at the Sorbonne, and together they developed the philosophical system of Existentialism. Author of many novels and the ground-breaking study The Second Sex, *de Beauvoir gave her weighty intellectual backing to many political campaigns, including the pro-abortion movement, and the French anti-war stance.*

Her relationship with Sartre, which endured for fifty years, obeyed its own, well-established rules. Both vowed to maintain their love affair as the central 'necessary' commitment, but to allow each other to have other 'contingent' liaisons as and when these surfaced. They seemed to surface often. For example, Sartre began an affair with a pupil, 'Olga D', who later formed an intense triangular friendship with him and de Beauvoir, then married Sartre's good friend Bost, another of de Beauvoir's conquests. Another lover whom both Sartre and de Beauvoir wooed and won was Louise Védrine, a young woman who was often discussed in intimate detail by the pair.

In practice it seems that Sartre's infidelities caused de Beauvoir some pain (detailed in her autobiographical novel A Woman Destroyed*), but in the following letter, written to Sartre during the war, while he was stationed in Alsace, de Beauvoir energetically describes her encounter with Bost to him with the candour which was the touchstone of this 'necessary love'.* *(See also* ***Desolation****.)*

To Jean-Paul Sartre

Hôtel de la gare
Albertville (Savoie)
Albertville, Wednesday [27 July 1938]

Dear little being,
I'm not going to write you a long letter, though I've hundreds of things to tell you, because I prefer to tell you them in person on Saturday. You should know, however:

1. First, that I love you dearly – I'm quite overcome at the thought that I'll see you disembarking from the train on Saturday, carrying your suitcase and my red hatbox – I can already picture us ensconced on our deckchairs overlooking a lovely blue sea and talking nineteen to the dozen – and I feel a great sense of well-being.

2. You've been very sweet to write me such long letters. I'm hoping for another this evening at Annecy. You tell me countless pleasing little items of news, but the most pleasing of all is that you've found your subject. The big page looks extremely fine with that title, just the perverse kind you like: *Lucifer* – I can find no fault with it.

3. Something extremely agreeable has happened to me, which I didn't at all expect when I left – I slept with Little Bost three days ago. It was I who propositioned him, of course. Both of us had been wanting it: we'd have serious conversations during the day, and the evenings would be unbearably oppressive. One rainy evening at Tignes, in a barn, lying face down a few inches away from one another, we gazed at each other for an hour finding various pretexts to put off the moment of going to sleep, he babbling frantically, I racking my brains vainly for the casual, appropriate words I couldn't manage to articulate – I'll tell you it all properly later. In the end I laughed foolishly and looked at him, so he said: 'Why are you laughing?' and I said: 'I'm trying to picture your face if I propositioned you to sleep with me' and he said: 'I was thinking that you were thinking that I wanted to kiss you but didn't dare.' After that we floundered on for another quarter of an hour before he made up his mind to kiss me. He was tremendously astonished when I told him I'd always had a soft spot for him – and he ended up telling me yesterday evening that he'd loved me for ages. I'm very fond of him. We spend idyllic days, and nights of passion. But have no fear of finding me sullen or disoriented or ill at ease on Saturday; it's something precious to me, something intense, but also light and easy and properly in its place in my life, simply a happy blossoming of relations that I'd always found very agreeable. It strikes me as funny, on the other hand, to think that I'm now going to spend two days with Védrine.

Goodbye, dear little being – I'll be on the platform on Saturday, or at the buffet if you don't see me on the platform. I'd like to spend long weeks alone with you. A big kiss.

Your Beaver

Translated by Quintin Hoare

ANON., POLITICAL PRISONER
(20th Century)
USSR

Letter to a lover from prison

Greetings, my darling.
God, where did you find such a marvellous Omar Khayyám saying? I wander around the compound like a shadow of myself, saying over and over again:

> In ocean depths concealed,
> The kernels ripen, shell-imprisoned.
> Now is the time, o pearls,
> For you to glimpse the light.

I told you the story once of how it came about that you fell in love with me, didn't I? Well, if not, now is the time. Listen.

A month after you appeared on the scene, when we had already become friends, I suddenly thought to myself: 'Why does he just keep on looking at me in that brotherly way? There's something wrong!' The fact that other people we had got to know took us for brother and sister pleased me, of course, but. . . . As our unfavourite poet Mayakovsky said: 'We women are trollops and wagtails, all of us.' And then one evening I invited a few friends around, you and some other artists, and instead of my everlasting threadbare jeans and my boring old sweater I put on a long velvet dress and put my hair up. And I might as well be completely honest about it – I went to town with the make-up, remorselessly using up a month's worth of expensive foreign cosmetics. That evening a cloth was carefully laid on the table to match my dress, candles were flickering, and appropriate background music was chosen – harpsichord. I made conversation with everyone in a soft, gentle voice, mentioning not a word either about my 'love' for Sofia Vlasyevna,* or about our recent hunger-strike (the couple of kilogrammes lost during that period now came in very handy), and at the end of the evening managed to arrange for N. to ask me to sing Pasternak's 'Winter's Night'. That was when you finally swallowed the bait, my poor little carp, my defenceless little fish!

*Sofya Vlasyevna – a humorous allegorical name based on the first syllables of the phrase 'Sovetskaya Vlast' (Soviet Power).

It's true, though. That's how it happened, isn't it? Well, I don't deny it, I don't deny that afterwards I fell head over heels in love with you, although at the beginning I was only trying to regulate the status quo of my little kingdom: i.e. please be at least a little bit in love with me! I must confess that in those days I used to love having someone around who was a little bit in love with me, just a tiny bit; not enough to be a burden, but someone I could be certain of, all the same. Who could have known that on this occasion I would fall for the bait myself? Otherwise I would just have gone on wearing my old sweater, and you wouldn't be writing to me now, across so many thousands of kilometres, about your love. You're a mercurial species, you men, that's all I have to say to you, darling!

My God, what are they doing to us women? Dear God, what is happening? After all, I would so like to spend my life sewing beautiful, dainty dresses for myself – I really enjoy sewing, embroidery, knitting – and giving birth to children one after the other, and writing poetry, clear simple verse for children and grown-up children. And better than anything, write fairy stories. Do you know that I have a whole book of rhyming fairytales which I show to no one – especially in these bleak times of ours! They would all burst out laughing! Instead I have to rush off to unofficial art exhibitions that are about to be smashed up, arrange hunger-strikes, tear myself away at any time of day or night and speed away to Moscow 'for the truth', that's to say, talk to the foreign correspondents. And I have to wear the most suitable clothes for such affairs and forgo everything which has to be renounced in this country in order not to lose the most important things of all: freedom and honour. Inner freedom I mean, of course (and that's another paradox: in order to secure inner freedom you are bound to have to pay with external freedom, but I suppose we all knew that). And now? No, my darling court-painter, I have deceived you – these wrinkles will never be smoothed out, I know that. And what about my toes? Can you imagine what they look like now after wearing these damned boots? You see, they're the kind of boots that soldiers have to wear, privates in the infantry! I hold my head high – after all, my status obliges me to do so – but what about my shoulders, will they ever stop being hunched? And my hands? They have become quite swarthy, and the skin has gone thin and is furrowed with tiny wrinkles. Do you still remember the candles, the poetry, the song to words by Pasternak. . . . We struggle for beauty in life and yet become ugly ourselves in the struggle. When you see me, you will be disappointed. Perhaps, what you love in me is the ghost of those happy days, and then this severe-looking female convict will appear before you. . . Try to have patience, and don't be disappointed right away, OK? Time will pass, and I will become very nice, peaceable, good-natured, quiet and cosy. We'll get things together!

Translated by Julia Voznesenskaya

MARY BICKNELL (1796–1828)
England

Mary Bicknell was engaged to the painter John Constable, something her father vehemently disapproved of, fearing (quite rightly, as it turned out) that Constable would be poor for a very long time. In her letters to Constable Bicknell seems to be trying to appease both father and fiancé, and succeeding with neither. She did marry Constable eventually, some five years later, in 1816.

To John Constable

Spring Grove,
November 4, 1811

My dear Sir, – I have just received my father's letter. It is precisely such a one as I expected, reasonable and kind; his only objection would be on the score of that necessary evil money. What can we do? I wish I had it, but wishes are vain: we must be wise, and leave off a correspondence that is not calculated to make us think less of each other. We have many painful trials required of us in this life, and we must learn to bear them with resignation. You will still be my friend, and I will be yours; then as such let me advise you to go into Suffolk, you cannot fail to be better there. I have written to papa, though I do not in conscience think that he can retract anything he has said, if so, I had better not write to you any more, at least till I can coin. We should both of us be bad subjects for poverty, should we not? Even painting would go on badly, it could hardly survive in domestic worry.

By a sedulous attention to your profession you will very much help to bestow calm on my mind. . . . You will allow others to outstrip you, and then perhaps blame me. Exert yourself while it is yet in your power, the path of duty is alone the path of happiness. . . . Believe me, I shall feel a more lasting pleasure in knowing that you are improving your time, than I should do while you were on a stolen march with me round the Park. Still I am not heroine enough to say, wish, or mean that we should never meet. I know that to be impossible. But then, let us resolve it shall be but seldom; not as inclination, but as prudence shall dictate. Farewell, dearest John – may every blessing attend you, and in the interest I feel in your welfare, forgive the advice I have given you, who, I am sure are better qualified to admonish me. Resolution is, I think, what we now stand most in need of, to refrain for a time, for our mutual good, from the society of each other.

Sept. 15, 1816

Papa is averse to everything I propose. If you please you may write to him; it will do neither good nor harm. I hope we are not going to do a very foolish thing. . . . Once more, and for the last time! it is not too late to follow Papa's advice, and *wait.* Notwithstanding all I have been writing, whatever you deem best I do. . . . This enchanting weather gives me spirits.

ELIZABETH SHERIDAN (1754–92)
England

In 1772, Miss Linley of Bath was a famous and glamorous opera singer of eighteen. The story is that one night Richard Brinsley Sheridan saw her at the theatre and fell instantly in love with her. After various exciting escapades involving duels and elopements, they were married in 1773. Her letters to Sheridan are written after three years of marriage, when some of the thrills of their whirlwind courtship seem to have given way to jealousies and loneliness.

To Richard Brinsley Sheridan

(1776)

My dearest love, – nothing can equal my disappointment on receiving your note. We expected you last night, and sat up till two this morning, and waited dinner till five today. I wish that, instead of Ned, you had sent the horses, that we might have come to you, for I almost despair of seeing you tomorrow at Heston. Do you really long to see me? And has nothing but business detained you from me? Dear, dear, Sheri, don't be angry. I cannot love you and be perfectly satisfied at such a distance from you. I depended upon your coming tonight, and shall not recover my spirits till we meet. Pray send the horses tonight, that I may be able to sett off early tomorrow. The weather has been so bad we have not been able to stir out of the house, so that you may suppose we have been comfortably dull, and this additional mortification has made both Mary (Mrs Tickell) and myself so cross that, I believe, nobody would envy us our *tête-à-tête* tonight.

I wish I could share your vexations with you, my poor love; but indeed I do so in imagination, though I am afraid that will not lighten your burdens. But don't fret, my dearest, for, let what will happen, we must be happy, if I can believe your constant assurances of affection. I could draw such a picture of happiness of you that it would almost make me wish to overthrow all our present schemes of future affluence and grandeur.

(1776)

My dear Dick, – though I do not yet despair of seeing you tonight, I write for fear you should be unavoidably detained again, for I fretted very much last night that I had not done so, as I thought you would have liked to have received a 'fiff' from me this morning when it was too late to send you one. Your note from Sevenoaks found me alone in very bad spirits indeed. It comforted me a little, but I cannot be happy while you are otherwise, whatever you may think to the contrary.

MILEVA MARIĆ (1875–1948)
Serbia

'Johnnie' and 'Dollie' were the pen names of the great theorist and scientist Albert Einstein and his girlfriend (then wife), Mileva Marić, used in their correspondence in an attempt to ensure that the letter writers were never identified. In fact, these letters, translated from the German by Shawn Smith, were not published until 1992, and tell a fascinating story, shedding new light on the previously shadowy figure of Mileva Marić.

Marić met Einstein in 1897, when she was twenty-one and he was eighteen, and they were both studying Physics at the Swiss Federal Institute. Marić, the only young woman taking the class, clearly felt isolated and lacked a true appreciation of the remarkable talent she possessed. Einstein himself believed she was easily his equal: 'a creature . . . who is as strong and independent as I am'.

Unfortunately, this independence was soon curtailed when Marić found herself in 1898 unmarried, in the midst of exams, and pregnant. Once her daughter, Lieserl, was born she was an embarrassment to Einstein, and he counselled Marić to keep her a secret from the Institute. With much sadness Marić allowed her daughter to be given up for adoption. The couple did marry in 1903, and had another child, a boy. By that time Marić had failed her exams and given up all hope of graduating. In the first letter to Einstein, the 'worst of moods' she alludes to is brought on by failing her exams. The second letter contains one of the only references to Marić and Einstein's daughter; 'those awful times' being the moment when Marić is forced to leave the child.

They divorced after fifteen years of marriage.

To Albert Einstein

[Zurich, 3 May 1901]

My dear Johnnie,

I received your dear little letter today and was surprised to see that you hadn't received my letter of acceptance yet. Was it really lost, or did something else happen to it? But I hope you've received it in the meantime. I also wrote you a little card yesterday while in the worst of moods because of a letter I received. But when I read your letter today I became a bit more cheerful, since I see how much you love me, so I think we'll take that little trip after all. I'll arrive in Como then on Sunday morning at 5:00, because I can't afford to waste an entire day traveling a route I already know (aren't you surprised at what a good little sweetheart you have?). And either you will be at the train station already, which seems unlikely, or I'll expect you to be on the first train from Milan. Then we'll walk around part of the lake on foot, practicing our botany, chatting, and enjoying each other's company. – But darling, I need to know if I'll be taking the same route home so I can buy a round-trip ticket, because it's a shame to waste the money. Why didn't you write to Winterthur once more to ask about the teaching job? Maybe they think it is understood; you've been asked and have agreed, after all; or did they intend to write you once more?

And you have so much love for your Dollie, and you long for her so! She's always so happy with your little letters full of passionate love, showing her that you are once again her dear sweetheart, and my God! what sweet little kisses she's saved for you!

I can't wait until Sunday! There are only two days left now, so don't oversleep. Awaiting you with a thousand pleasures, your tormented

Dollie

[Stein am Rhein]
Wednesday [13 November 1901]

My dear, naughty little sweetheart,
Now you're not coming tomorrow again! And you don't even say: 'I'm coming on Sunday instead.' But then you'll surely surprise me, right? You know, if you don't come at all, I may just leave! If you only knew how terribly homesick I am you would surely come.

Are you really out of money? That's nice! The man earns 150 francs, has room and board provided, and at the end of the month doesn't have a cent to his name! What would people say? But don't ever again use that as an excuse for Sunday, please. If you don't get any money by then I'll send you some.

Is your cousin still staying with you? Did he find his ticket? Did he come especially to visit you? One doesn't usually go by way of Schaffhausen, and would normally avoid such a mishap!

There was a fair in Schaffhausen yesterday, but unfortunately I heard about it too late. Otherwise I would have come and bought you something nice, and looked at your tower, possibly spotting my dear little sweetheart in it. If you only knew how much I want to see you again! I think about you all day long, and even more at night, and when you tell me all sorts of sweet things, then I think about you even more.

I'm very curious about what Kleiner will say about the two papers. He should pull himself together and say something sensible. I'd be so happy if you could do the other one soon too.

I'm going to write to Helene. She's surely had her 'tiny one' by now. I haven't written her in such a long time because I just wasn't able to bring myself to do it in those awful times. I wrote a long letter once and poured my heart out to her, but then I tore it up. I'm glad I did so. I don't think we should say anything about Lieserl just now; but you should write her a few words every now and then. We must treat her well because she can help us with something important, but mainly because she's so nice and kind and would be so pleased, right, sweetheart? – I read the book by Forel. Stadler said that hypnotism is immoral, and when I read the book I had the same feeling of disgust. Suggestion certainly plays an important role in everything, and I even think that doctors should use it up to a certain point. But such a violation of human consciousness! I feel that Forel distinguishes himself from a quack only inasmuch as he faces his patients with more self-confidence, that is to say 'impertinence,' based on his more extensive knowledge. But people are such a stupid herd. – I don't understand hypnotic sleep, maybe it can't be understood at all, maybe it doesn't exist at all! I think this is suggestion as well, or at best autosuggestion, because I think most of the experiments he cites are dishonest (sorry!). I'll tell you why later.

But farewell for now, my little one, my darling. Do you think of me too sometimes, but nice, sweet thoughts? So you're coming on Sunday now, right, sweetheart? I've already saved up so many kisses that if the bowl overflows they'll all be gone. So for now, tender kisses and best wishes from your

Dollie

who is very angry with you right now.

I'll tell you a funny story about something that happened to you once.

Translated by Shawn Smith

ANAÏS NIN (1903–77)
USA

Poet, short-story writer, famous diarist – Nin is best known for The Diary of Anaïs Nin 1931–1977, *which appeared in seven volumes, and* Delta of Venus: Erotica (1977). *She also wrote many novels and essays, and was a practising psychoanalyst, having studied with Otto Rank.*

She writes here to the American writer Henry Miller, with whom she was conducting a complicated affair while still married to Hugh Guiler. Miller and Nin first met in Paris in 1931. Initially it was June, Miller's wife, with whom Nin fell in love, and a strong feature of Nin and Miller's relationship was a shared adulation of June.

Despite the protestations of the following letters from Nin to Miller, written just a year after their liaison began, neither party was able to leave their marriages until much later. Miller divorced June in 1934; Nin did not separate from Guiler until the late 1940s. By then the affair had cooled.

To Henry Miller

[Achensee]
[August 6, 1932]

Oh, Henry, I was so upset by your letter this morning. When it was given to me all the artificially pent-up feelings overwhelmed me. The very touch of the letter was as if you had taken me all into your arms. You know now what I felt when I read it. You said everything that would touch and win me and I was *moist*, and so impatient that I am doing *everything* to gain a day. This note I'm enclosing, which I wrote you last night two hours after mailing my letter, will help you to understand what is happening. Anyway you must have received the telegram almost at the same time. I belong to you! We're going to have a week such as we never dreamt yet. 'The thermometer will burst.' I want to feel again the violent thumping inside of me, the rushing, burning blood, the slow, caressing rhythm and the sudden violent pushing, the frenzy of pauses when I hear the raindrop sounds . . . how it leaps in my mouth, Henry. Oh, Henry, I can't bear to be writing you – I want you desperately, I want to open my legs so wide, I'm melting and palpitating. I want to do things so wild with you that I don't know how to say them.

Hugo is calling. I'll answer the rest of the letter tonight.

Anaïs

[Louveciennes]
[August 30, 1932]

Henry,
I am again coming out in the open. I do not want to see you for a few days. You have asked things of me which are *humanly* unbearable. You have asked me to thrive on a half love, and also to give you my understanding of June so that you could add this to yours and write your book out of both. I have wanted to give you the impossible, the gigantic, the inhuman. I thought I could stand the arrival of all these pages in which you do every day more justice to her wonder. You are testing my courage to the full, like a torturer. How to extricate myself from this nightmare? I have only one source of strength (*humanly*, I have no strength), I have only writing, and it is this which I am doing now with a desperation you can never conceive of – I am writing *against* myself, *against* what you call my imperfections, *against* the woman, *against* my humaneness, *against* the continents which are giving way. Two things may happen: in a few days I may be dauntless again, and you can go on with your interesting and monstrous experiments; or I may send you a postcard from Stamboul. Don't come and show me the immediacy of your *humaneness* – behind your humaneness there is always a great evaluator.

I may not send you this letter. I still have the instinct that the most important thing is your book, and that I must not disturb your work on that. The rest is just human life.

Anaïs

[Louveciennes]
Sept. 6, 1932

Henry,
you have just left. I told Hugh I had something to add to my work. I had to come upstairs [to] my room again, and be alone. I was so filled with you I was afraid to show my face. Henry, no departure of yours has ever left me so shattered. I don't know what it was tonight, which drew me to you, which made me frantic to stay close to you, to *sleep* with you, to hold you . . . a mad and terrific tenderness . . . a desire to care for you. . . . It was a great pain to me that you should be leaving. When you talk the way you talked about *Mädchen* [*in Uniform*], when you are thoughtful and moving, I lose my mind. To

stay with you for one night I would throw away my whole life, sacrifice a hundred persons, I would burn Louveciennes, be capable of *anything*. This is not to worry you, Henry, it is just that I can't keep from saying it, that I am overflowing, desperately in love with you as I never was with anyone. Even if you had left tomorrow morning the idea that you were sleeping in the same house would have been a very sweet relief from the torment I endure tonight, the torment of being cut in two pieces when you closed the gate behind you. Henry, Henry, Henry, I love you, love you, love you. I was jealous of [Jean] Renaud who has you all these days, who sleeps in Clichy. Tonight everything hurts, not only the separation, but this terrible hunger of body and mind for you which every day you are increasing, stirring more and more.' I don't know what I am writing. Feel me holding you as I have never held you before, more deeply, more sadly, more desperately, more passionately. I kneel before you, I give you myself and it is not enough, not enough. I adore you. Your body, your face, your voice, your human self, oh Henry, I can't go now and sleep in Hugh's arms – I can't. I want to run away just to be alone with my feelings for you.

Anaïs

MARIA DEL SOCORRO VARILLA DE VEGA
(Late 20th Century)
Mexico

There are an estimated 35 million Hispanic immigrants in the USA who are undocumented, and considered illegal. Many young men travel to California from Mexico, sending money home to their wives and girlfriends, hoping either to make enough money to return and start a new life in Mexico or, in time, to bring their families over to the States. In many cases, of course, the reunion never happens. Maria del Socorro, pregnant with her second child, sending letters from Mexico City to her lover in Los Angeles, is well aware of this. She writes with passion to the father of her children, Sergio Vega, who is due to return to Mexico in January.

To Sergio Vega (extract)

Socorro
Ciudad Netzahualcóyotl, Mexico City, Mexico
December 21, 1988

Sergio Vega
Los Angeles, CA

Love,
I hope you find yourself healthy, the same with all my brothers, these are my biggest wishes, well here we're well, anyway I'm as well as you can imagine with the normal little complaints of carrying a child, Boy, this very moment as I'm writing you your baby's moving and moving, it seems he knows what I'm feeling, and about Eric, he's going to school today, you know, he's crazy with his little sibling, get this, he takes good care of me and as you may recall he kisses my belly, now about my mom, she finds herself well, and about my papa, you already know he doesn't understand, he goes on the same, he goes on drinking, he comes home drunk and with his moods he's soon fighting with my mom, but I tell my mom not to pay attention to him, better that he sleep, and now My Heart I want you to know that I don't behave badly, I want you to tell me why you say this, you know that I don't think of anything else that's not related to you, or that quite the contrary, good, I hope that you are indeed complying with what you promised me just like I am, that we're going to respect and to wait, for my part, yes, I go on loving you the same if not more than ever, and more now that I'm not thinking bad

things, and I hope to God that I always go on loving you so much, you know, I've never stopped loving you, and more now, that you're everything, my being, my everything and my life, and that's why I want the time to pass quickly and then for us to be together forever.

MADAME ROLAND (1754–93)
France

Manon Jeanne Philipon, spirited, educated daughter of a Paris engraver, declared at eighteen that she was in need of a 'philosopher' for a husband. She believed she had found him in Jean-Marie Roland de la Platière. However, her wit, gaiety and robust appetites led her to seek pleasure with many other men, one of them the deputy Léonard Buzot, to whom she is writing here, from prison.

The setting is the French Revolution; Madame Roland's sentence is death by guillotine. She is said to have borne her fate with 'noble fortitude'.

To Léonard Buzot

(From prison) June 22nd, 1793

How often do I not re-read your letters! I press them to my heart, I cover them with my kisses. I did not expect any more. Without success I asked for news of you from Madame Cholet. I wrote once to M. le Tellier in Evreux, so that you should receive a sign of life from me, but the postal connection is interrupted. I did not want to send you anything direct, because your name would suffice for the letter to be intercepted, and I might besides attract suspicion to you. Proud and calm I came here, with wishes for the defenders of liberty and some hopes for them. When I heard of the decree of arrest that had been promulgated against the twenty-two, I exclaimed 'My country is lost.' I remained in painful anxiety, before I had certain news of your flight, and the decree issued for your arrest frightens me anew.

This horrible thing is no doubt due to your courage; since I know that you are in the Calvados, I regain my equanimity. Continue in your noble endeavours, my friend. Brutus despaired too soon of the Roman safety at the battle of Philippi. As long as a republican still breathes, is free, has his courage, he must, he can be useful. The south of France offers you in any case a refuge, and will be the asylum of honourable men. Thither you must turn your looks and wend your steps. There you will have to live, in order to serve your fellows and to exercise your virtues.

I personally shall know how to wait quietly, until the reign of justice returns, or shall undergo the last acts of violence, of tyranny in such a manner, that my example too will not be without utility. . . .

LADY MARY WORTLEY MONTAGU (1689–1762)
England

Letter writer, dramatist, commentator, poet and Whig polemicist. Born into an aristocratic family, she began writing poetry at the age of fourteen. After a tortuous courtship she eloped with Edward Wortley Montagu in 1712. Despite the lengths needed to secure the marriage, it proved unfulfilling.

To Edward Wortley Montagu

[25th April 1710]

I have this minute receivd your 2 Letters. I know not how to direct to you, whether to London or the country, or if in the country to Durham or Wortley. Tis very likely you'l never receive this. I hazard a great deal if it falls into other hands, and I write for all that –

I wish with all my soul I thought as you do. I endeavor to convince my selfe by your Arguments, and am sorry my reason is so obstinate not to be deluded into an Opinion that tis impossible a Man can esteem a Woman. I suppose I should then be very easy at your thoughts of me. I should thank you for the wit and Beauty you give me and not be angry at the follys and weaknesses, but to my Infinite affliction I can beleive neither one nor tother. One part of my Character is not so good nor th'other so bad as you fancy it. Should we ever live together you would be disapointed both ways; you would find an easy equality of temper you do not expect, and a thousand faults you do not imagine. You think if you marry'd me I should be passionately fond of you one month and of some body else the next. Neither would happen. I can esteem, I can be a freind, but I don't know whether I can Love. Expect all that is complaisant and easy, but never what is fond in me. You Judge very wrong of my Heart when you suppose me capable of veiws of Interest, and that any thing could oblige me to flatter any body. Was I the most indigent Creature in the world I should answer you as I do now, without adding or deminishing. I am incapable of Art, and 'tis because I will not be capable of it. Could I deceive one minute, I should never regain my own good Opinion, and who could bear to live with one they despis'd?

If you can resolve to live with a Companion that will have all the deference due to your superiority of good sense, and that your proposals can be agreable to those on whom I depend – I have nothing to say against them.

As to travelling, tis what I should doe with great pleasure, and could easily quit London upon your account, but a retirement in the country is not so disagreable to me, as I know a few months would make it tiresome to you. Where people are ty'd for Life, tis their mutual Interest not to grow weary of one Another. If I had all the personal charms that I want, a Face is too slight a foundation for happynesse. You would be soon tir'd with seeing every day the same thing, where you saw nothing else. You would have leisure to remark all the defects, which would encrease in proportion as the novelty lessend, which is allwaies a great charm. I should have the displeasure of seeing a coldnesse, which tho' I could not reasonably blame you for, being involuntary, yet it would render me uneasy, and the more because I know a Love may be reviv'd which Absence, Inconstancy, or even Infidelity has extinguish'd, but there is no returning from a degout given by Satiety.

I should not chuse to live in a croud. I could be very well pleasd to be in London without makeing a great Figure or seeing above 8 or 9 agreable people. Apartments, Table, etc. are things that never come into my head. But [I] will never think of any thing without the consent of my Family, and advise you not to fancy a happynesse in entire solitude, which you would find only Fancy.

Make no an[swer t]o this. If you can like me on my own terms, tis not to me you must make your proposals. If not, to what purpose is our Correspondance?

However, preserve me your Freindship, which I think of with a great deal of pleasure and some Vanity. If ever you see me marry'd, I flatter my selfe you'l see a Conduct you would not be sorry your Wife should Imitate.

[15th August 1712]
Friday night

I tremble for what we are doing. Are you sure you will love me for ever? Shall we never repent? I fear, and I hope. I foresee all that will happen on this Occassion. I shall incense my Familly [to] the highest degree. The gennerallity of the World will blame my conduct, and the Relations and freinds of—will invent a thousand storyes of me, yet – tis possible you may recompense every thing to me. In this Letter (which I am fond of) you promise me all that I wish. Since I writ so far, I receiv'd your friday Letter. I will be only yours, and I will do what you please. (Postscript) You shall hear from me again to morrow, not to contradict but to give Some directions. My resolution is taken – Love me and use me well.

[16th August 1712]
Satterday Morning

I writ you a Letter last night in some passion. I begin to fear again; I own my selfe a coward. – You made no reply to one part of my Letter concerning my Fortune. I am afraid you flatter your selfe that my F[ather] may be at length reconcile'd and brought to reasonable terms. I am convince'd by what I have often heard him say, speaking of other cases like this, he never will. The fortune he has engag'd to give with me was settle'd, on my B[rother's] marriage, on my sister and my selfe, but in such a manner that it was left in his power to give it all to either of us, or divide it as he thought fit. He has given it all to me. Nothing remains for my sister but the free bounty of my F[ather] from what he can save, which notwithstanding the greatnesse of his Estate may be very little. Possibly after I have disoblig'd him so much, he may be glad to have her so easily provided for, with Money allready rais'd, especially if he has a design to marry him selfe, as I hear.

I do not speak this that you should not endeavor to come to terms with him, if you please, but I am fully perswaded it will be to no purpose. He will have a very good Answer to make, that I suffer'd this Match to proceed, that I made him a very silly figure in it, that I have let him spend £400 in wedding cloaths, all which I saw without saying any thing. When I first pretended to oppose this Match, he told me he was sure I had some other design in my head. I deny'd it with truth, but you see how little appearance there is of that Truth. He proceeded with telling me that he would never enter into treaty with another Man, etc., and that I should be sent immediately into the North, to stay there, and when he dy'd he would only leave me an Annuity of £400.

I had not courrage to stand this Vein, and I submitted to what he pleas'd. He will now object against me, why, since I intended to marry in this Manner, I did not persist in my first resolution? that it would have been as easy for me to run away from T[horesby] as from hence, and to what purpose did I put him and the Gentleman I was to marry for Expense etc.? He will have a thousand plausible reasons for being irreconcilable, and tis very probable the World will be on his Side. – Refflect now for the last time in what manner you must take me. I shall come to you with only a Nightgown and petticoat, and this is all you will get with me.

I have told a Lady of my Freinds what I intend to do. You will think her a very good Freind when I tell you she has proffer'd to lend us her house, if we would come there the first Night. I did not accept of this, till I had let you know it. If you think it more convenient to carry me to your Lodging, make no scrupule of it. Let it be what it will, if I am your Wife, I shall think no place unfit for me where you are. I beg we may leave London next morning, where ever you intend to go. I should wish to go out of England if it suits with your Affairs. You are the best Judge of your father's temper. If you think it would be obliging to him, or necessary for you, I will go with you immediately to ask his pardon and his blessing. If that is not proper at first, [I] think the best Scheme is going to the Spaw. When you come back you may endeavor to Make your Father admit of seeing me, and treat with mine (tho' I persist in thinking it will be to no purpose). But I cannot think of living in the midst of my Relations and Acquaintance after so unjustifiable a step – unjustifiable to the World. – But I think I can justify my selfe to my selfe. –

LADY MARY ELCHO (1866–1914)
England

An Edwardian socialite, Lady Mary Elcho, née *Wyndham, married to Hugo Elcho, was the long-standing confidante and 'companion' of Arthur Balfour, Conservative MP and Prime Minister between 1902 and 1906.*

Lady Elcho's reputation did not seem to suffer as a result of her friendship with Balfour, which spanned forty years, in the days when the Gentlemen of the Press maintained a discreet silence about the affairs of government Ministers. Her letter to Balfour demonstrates her sense of humour and the joy she took in reliving the submissive moments of the man who has been called Britain's worst Prime Minister of the twentieth century.

To Arthur Balfour

Abbey Leix
30 October 1903

. . . It amuses me to think of you as a sun with those worshipping female planets, those sisters of yrs revolving round you, their adoring interest centred on you, I long to be there always to keep you in yr place.

I should make you happier in some ways but I should be stricter and I should make you have yr guests for 2 nights not *one*; *you* seem to think some things are better 2 nights than one! They are so afraid of boring you and so anxious to keep you to themselves. . . .

Goodnight

Melcho

In a train between Oxford and Warwick
19 January 1904

I was overwhelmed with depression at leaving you Sunday night, and I think you looked rather sad too which – this sounds unkind – was rather a consolation. It was horrid leaving at that hour but practically it was unavoidable so 'there's nothing to regret' in *that* sense (this is a Whitt phrase) except that it had to be done and I think it was quite clever of me to fit in everything so well and manage to get to you – you see, I felt it my duty to put you in *yr place* (on yr knees at my feet) and *that* I flatter myself I have thoroughly done. Sunday was a little disappointing, because altho' my conscience wanted you to go to church I *should* have liked to have had some fun with you in the morning. I was in great spirits and full of mischief when you rushed in. (By the way, how *awful* of you to leave my letter in yr room) then came the long walk and one hour in yr room seemed very little in all the day and it was wasted in talking business. 2 hrs is what I like: one for boring things and one for putting you in yr place: I know I dwell too much on each thing and the more I fancy you're bored the more gingerly I go, which is quite wrong. I hate rushing but it ought to be done as time is short. Then the interval between tea and dinner and departure was a great strain because I felt I wanted so to see you alone and kept *wondering* if it could be managed somehow but it couldn't be managed, certainly not unless I had arranged it beforehand – impossible to get yr attention, I thought of yr showing me something or fetching something in yr room. Eventually I gave it up and mental and physical spirits went down like a pricked balloon. I had some of my pain in my side. The motor drive was very nice but not so much fun *going away* in it. I tipped Mills. . . .

I wish I had a motor. I forgot to tell you that Tuesday 6th would suit me best: I should like a clear week at Stanway but you must settle what pleases you. Goodbye. Bless you.

ME

I hope you are all right? Destroy.

JUNE JORDAN (*b.* 1936)
USA

June Jordan was born in Harlem and raised in Brooklyn, where she began writing poetry at the age of seven. Her writing has won her much acclaim and many literary awards. Work includes His Own Where *(a novel),* Moving Towards Home *and* Technical Difficulties *(political essays),* Lyrical Campaigns, *and* Haruko/Love Poetry. *She lives in California.*

Letter to Haruko From Decorah, Iowa, USA

In this white space this American
page of immigration from three months
of darkness in Norway/hunger
unrelieved by sun or flowerlight
or playful ambulations through an easy
day
I stand beside a stranger
ice and snow stretched pale for miles
behind me
village streets bare/no
trees/pedestrians/dogs/or shadow
on the hard brick of the local
will to persevere
to stay until the whisperings of spring arrive
to marry
to bake bread
to break a window out of solid log
cabin walls that wheeze with winter
inescapable

A stranger points to handicrafts
traditional
in hand-hewn pine and homemade paints
that sanctify a bed a chair a bowl
with hours of devotion
agitant against a loneliness as unmistakable
as thirst or sex
and I am taken by these florid
refutations of a frozen near horizon

brilliant tokens of a flesh soft loom that held
some woman's sanity together
ravelling intelligence
like thread that magical
became a cloth
of loving color

And I am straining to converge
this plain
midwestern/fasting stand of oak trees
quiet as they ramify
in such thin air
with your true
handheld miracles of rain
your expert
California camera capturing
a lush a sudden deluge
from an otherwise
dry sky

But the roots
for a connection that can keep
Japan and San Francisco
and Jamaica and Decorah
Iowa and Norway
all in one place palpable
to any sweet belief
move deep below
apparent differences of turf

I trace them in the lifeline
of an open palm
a hand that works
its homemade heat
against the jealous
hibernating blindness
of the night
plum blossom plum jam
even the tree becomes something
more than a skeleton
longing for the sky

CONSUMMATION:
'Love me and use me well'

VIRGINIA WOOLF (1882–1941)
England

(See also **Initiation**, **Declaration**, **Desolation** and **Celebration**.)

To Vita Sackville-West

52 Tavistock Square
Sunday [7 October]

Dearest Creature,
It was a very very nice letter you wrote by the light of the stars at midnight. Always write then, for your heart requires moonlight to deliquesce it. And mine is fried in gaslight, as it is only nine o'clock and I must go to bed at eleven. And so I shant say anything: not a word of the balm to my anguish – for I am always anguished – that you were to me. How I watched you! How I felt – now what was it like? Well, somewhere I have seen a little ball kept bubbling up and down on the spray of a fountain: the fountain is you; the ball me. It is a sensation I get only from you. It is physically stimulating, restful at the same time. . . .

Berg

ELIZABETH BARRETT BROWNING (1806–61)
England

The most respected and successful woman poet of the Victorian era, a serious contender for the laureateship which eventually went to Tennyson in 1850. Her epic poem Aurora Leigh *(1857) is probably her major achievement, along with the celebrated sequence of love lyrics* Sonnets from the Portuguese.

Her legendary romance with Robert Browning sprang from a love letter he wrote to her in 1845. A year later she ran away from her tyrannical father to marry him in secret. The couple left immediately for Italy, and based themselves in Florence for the rest of Barrett's life.

In the first letter Barrett discusses the wedding plans; in the second they have been secretly married and are awaiting their escape to Italy.

To Robert Browning

[September 1846]

Dearest take this word, as if it were many. I am so tired – and then it shall be the right word.

Sunday and Friday are impossible. On Saturday I will go to you, if you like – with half done, – nothing done – scarcely. Will you come for me to Hodgson's? or shall I meet you at the station? At what o'clock should I set out, to be there at the hour you mention?

Also, for the boxes – we cannot carry them out of the house, you know, Wilson and I. They must be sent on Friday evening to the Vauxhall station, 'to be taken care of.' Will the people keep them carefully? Ought someone to be spoken to beforehand? If we sent them to New Cross, they would not reach you in time.

Hold me my beloved – with your love. It is very hard – But Saturday seems the only day for us. Tell me if you think so indeed.

Your very own BA

Sunday [Postmark, September 14, 1846]

My Own Beloved, if ever you should have reason to complain of me in things voluntary and possible, all other women would have a right to tread me underfoot, I should be so vile and utterly unworthy. There is my answer to what you wrote yesterday of wishing to be better to me . . . you! What could be better than lifting me from the ground and carrying me into life and the sunshine? I was yours rather by right than by gift (yet by gift also, my beloved!); for what you have saved and renewed is surely yours. All that I am, I owe you – if I enjoy anything now and henceforth, it is through you. You know this well. Even as *I*, from the beginning, knew that I had no power against you . . . or that, if I *had* it was for your sake.

Dearest, in the emotion and confusion of yesterday morning, there was yet room in me for one thought which was not a feeling – for I thought that, of the many, many women who have stood where I stood, and to the same end, not one of them all perhaps, not one perhaps, since that building was a church, has had reasons strong as mine, for an absolute trust and devotion towards the man she married, – not one! And then I both thought and felt, that it was only just, for them . . . those women who were less happy, . . . to have that affectionate sympathy and support and presence of their nearest relations, parent or sister . . . which failed to *me*, . . . needing it less through being happier!

All my brothers have been here this morning, laughing and talking, and discussing this matter of the leaving town, – and in the room, at the same time, were two or three female friends of ours, from Herefordshire – and I did not dare to cry out against the noise, though my head seemed splitting in two (one-half for each shoulder), I had such a morbid fear of exciting a suspicion. Treppy too being one of them, I promised to go to see her tomorrow and dine in her drawing-room if she would give me, for dinner, some bread and butter. It was like having a sort of fever. And all in the midst, the bells began to ring. 'What bells are those?' asked one of the provincials. 'Marylebone Church bells,' said Henrietta, standing behind my chair.

And now . . . while I write, having escaped from the great din, and sit here quietly, – comes . . . who do you think? – Mr Kenyon.

He came with his spectacles, looking as if his eyes reached to their rim all the way round; and one of the first words was, '*When did you see Browning?*' And I think I shall make a pretension to presence of mind henceforward; for, though *certainly* I changed colour and he saw it, I yet answered with a tolerably quick evasion, . . . 'He was here on Friday' – and leapt straight into another subject, and left him gazing fixedly on my face. Dearest, he saw something, but not all. So we talked, talked. He told me that the 'Fawn of Sertorius' (which I refused to cut open the other day) was ascribed to Landor and he told me that he meant to leave town again on Wednesday, and would see me once more before then. On rising to go away, he mentioned your name a second time . . . 'When do you see Browning again?' To which I answered that I did not know.

Is not *that* pleasant? The worst is that all these combinations of things make me feel so bewildered that I cannot make the necessary arrangements, as far as the letters go. But I must break from the dream-stupor which falls on me when left to myself a little, and set about what remains to be done.

A house near Watford is thought of now – but, as none is concluded on, the removal is not likely to take place in the middle of the week even, perhaps.

I sit in a dream, when left to myself. I cannot believe, or understand. Oh! but in all this difficult, embarrassing and painful situation, I look over the palms to Troy – I feel happy and exulting to belong to you, past every opposition, out of sight of every will of man – none can put us asunder, now, at least. I have a right now openly to love you, and to hear other people call it a *duty*, when I do, . . . knowing that if it were a sin, it would be done equally. Ah – I shall not be the first to leave off *that* – see if I shall! May God bless you, ever and ever dearest! Beseech for me the indulgence of your father and mother, and ask your sister to love me. I feel so as if I had slipped down over the wall into somebody's garden – I feel ashamed. To be grateful and affectionate to them all, while I live; is all that I can do, and it is too much a matter of course to need to be promised. Promise it however for your very own Ba whom you made so happy with the dear letter last night. But say in the next how you are – and how your mother is.

I did hate so, to have to take off the ring. You will have to take the trouble of putting it on again, some day.

NKWETO WA CHILINDA (*b.* 1949)
Zambia/England

Nkweto wa Chilinda lives and works in Britain. This letter marked the beginning of a dramatic six-month affair with a 'small island man' (her words), who lives and works in Amsterdam.

After the initial consummation, detailed here, the relationship was conducted across an ocean, in letters and via the telephone. He never replied to the numerous (sometimes three a week) letters that Chilinda wrote to him . . . preferring the telephone, protesting that he was intimidated by her writing style.

Mpenzi (extract)

7th December 1991

Mpenzi . . .
I'm writing this on the train because I have a feeling that when I get back to the routine of home, I won't be able to say what I want . . . to remember you as I want to . . . to remember the last three nights and days . . . to remember your hands on my body and to feel you in my body. . . .

I don't think I'll ever forget the expression on your face when I said, 'I'll buy you a drink . . .' knowing I wanted you then . . . in those first moments when I came up to you on the (deliberately transparent) excuse of asking for a copy of your paper. . . . And your first words to me exposing the excuse . . . 'you know I don't have a written paper . . . I said that at the beginning of my talk!' And later in the pub with your friends watching the scene unfold right before their eyes . . . your hand under the table caressing my thighs most of the night . . . I must have had a demented expression on my face as I was slowly losing my mind. . . . And later still arriving at my friend's house (having warned her I was bringing *a friend* back, and she, assuming a female friend!) . . . and the, seemingly long wait to get into my single bed. . . .

So . . . mpenzi . . . (this will be your first word in Kiswahili). . . . Mpenzi is a wonderful word because it encompasses all those that we love . . . it can mean 'lover' in the English way . . . but it can also mean 'loved one', which is the one I want for you, because although you have become my lover . . . you are a loved one to me. . . .

Your second (and last word for now) is . . . Tutaonana . . . Which

I'll use at the end of the letter . . . again the simple translation would be . . . 'see you' . . . but there is a certainty in that word that cannot be translated. It is, in fact, a statement of *fact.* WE WILL SEE EACH OTHER AGAIN . . . as we must if I don't want to go completely insane. . . . And, yes . . . I will arrange for you to fly back to the UK in January . . . when the mess of the Xmas break is over . . . (I wasn't joking). . . . In the meantime . . . I look forward to getting home and to your call before you leave for Amsterdam. . . . Don't forget my body too soon . . . mpenzi . . . I still remember your hands giving me a bath on that first morning . . . I better stop, as we are nearly there. . . .

Mpenzi . . . Tutaonana . . .
All my love. . . .

EMILY DICKINSON (1830–86)
USA

(See also **Invitation**, **Adulation**, **Celebration**.)

To Susan Gilbert (Dickinson)

late April 1852

So sweet and still, and Thee, Oh Susie, what need I more, to make my heaven whole?

Sweet Hour, blessed Hour, to carry me to you, and to bring you back to me, long enough to snatch one kiss, and whisper Goodbye, again.

I have thought of it all day, Susie, and I fear of but little else, and when I was gone to meeting it filled my mind so full, I could not find a *chink* to put the worthy pastor; when he said 'Our Heavenly Father,' I said 'Oh Darling Sue'; when he read the 100th Psalm, I kept saying your precious letter all over to myself, and Susie, when they sang – it would have made you laugh to hear one little voice, piping to the departed. I made up words and kept singing how I loved you, and you had gone, while all the rest of the choir were singing Hallelujahs. I presume nobody heard me, because I sang *so small*, but it was a kind of a comfort to think I might put them out, singing of you. I a'nt there this afternoon, tho', because I am here, writing a little letter to my dear Sue, and I am very happy. I think of ten weeks – Dear One, and I think of love, and you, and my heart grows full and warm, and my breath stands still. The sun does'nt shine at all, but I can feel a sunshine stealing into my soul and making it all summer, and every thorn, a *rose*. And I pray that each summer's sun shine on my Absent One, and cause her bird to sing!

You have been happy, Susie, and now are sad – and the whole world seems lone; but it wont be so always, 'some days *must* be dark and dreary'! You wont cry any more, will you, Susie, for my father will be your father, and my home will be your home, and where you go, I will go, and we will lie side by side in the kirkyard.

I have parents on earth, dear Susie, but your's are in the skies, and I have an earthly fireside, but you have one above, and you have a 'Father in Heaven,' where I have *none* – and *sister* in heaven, and I know they love you dearly, and think of you every day.

Oh I wish I had half so many dear friends as you in heaven – I could'nt spare them now – but to know they had got there safely, and should suffer nevermore – Dear Susie!

I know I was very naughty to write such fretful things, and I know I could have helped it, if I had tried hard enough, but I thought my heart would break, and I knew of nobody here that cared anything about it – so I said to myself, 'We will tell Susie about it.' You dont know what a comfort it was, and you wont know, till the big cup of bitterness is filled brimfull, and they say, 'Susie, drink it!' Then Darling, let me be there, and let me drink the half, and you will feel it all!

I am glad you have rested, Susie. I wish the week had been *more*, a whole *score* of days and joys for you, yet again, had it lasted longer, then had you not come so soon and I had been lonelier, it is right as it is! Ten weeks, they will seem short to you – for care will fill them, but to Mattie and me, long. We shall grow tired, waiting, and our eyes will ache with looking for you, and with now and then a tear. And yet we have *hope* left, and we shall keep her busy, cheering away the time. Only think Susie, it is vacation now – there shall be no more vacation until ten weeks have gone, and no more snow; and how very little while it will be now, before you and I are sitting out on the broad stone step, mingling our lives together! I cant talk of it now tho', for it makes me long and yearn so, that I cannot sleep tonight, for thinking of it, and you.

Yes, we did go sugaring, and remembered who was gone – and who was there last year, and love and recollection brought with them Little Regret, and set her in the midst of us.

Dear Susie, Dear Joseph; why take the best and dearest, and leave our hearts behind? While the Lovers sighed; and twined oak leaves, and the *anti* enamored ate sugar, and crackers, in the house, I went to see what I could find. Only think of it, Susie; I had'nt any appetite, nor any Lover, either, so I made the best of fate, and gathered antique stones, and your little flowers of moss opened their lips and spoke to me, so I was not alone, and bye and bye Mattie and me might have been seen sitting together upon a high – gray rock, and we might have been heard talking, were anyone very near! And did thoughts of that dear Susie go with us on the rock, and sit there 'tween us twain? Loved One, thou knowest!

I gathered something for you, because you were not there, an acorn, and some moss blossoms, and a little shell of a snail, so whitened by the snow you would think 'twas a cunning artist had carved it from alabaster – then I tied them all up in a leaf with some last summer's grass I found by a brookside, and I'm keeping them all for you.

I saw Mattie at church today, tho' could not speak to her. Friday evening I saw her, and talked with her besides. Oh I do love her – and when you come if we all live till then, it will be *precious*, Susie. You speak to me of sorrow, of what you have 'lost and loved,' say rather, of what you have loved and *won*, for it is *much*, dear Susie; I can count the big, true hearts by *clusters*, full of bloom, and bloom amaranthine, because *eternal*!

Emilie –

I have heard all about the journal. Oh Susie, that you should come to this! I want you to get it bound – at my expense – Susie – so when he takes you from me, to live in his new home, I may have *some* of you. I am sincere.

Mother sends her best love to you. It makes her look so happy when I give your's to her. Send it always, Susie, and send your respects to father! And much from Vinnie. She was so happy at her note. After she finished reading it, she said, 'I dont know but it's wrong, but I love Sue better – than Jane, and I love her and Mattie better than all the friends I ever had in my life.' Vinnie hopes to be like you, and to do as you do.

MARY WOLLSTONECRAFT (1759–97)
England

Mary Wollstonecraft was born in Hoxton, London. Her childhood was an unhappy one, dominated by an alcoholic father. At nineteen she earned her living as a governess; some years later she became literary adviser to Johnson, the publisher.

Wollstonecraft was a pioneer of women's rights. Her best-known work is A Vindication of the Rights of Woman, *which has become one of the most famous texts in English feminism. In 1792, the year of its publication, Wollstonecraft went to Paris and fell in love with Gilbert Imlay, becoming pregnant. This relationship was unhappy, and on her return to England she began to live with the anarchist philosopher William Godwin, whom she married in 1797, giving birth to a second child, Mary (who became Mary Shelley, author of* Frankenstein*). Wollstonecraft died a few days after Mary's birth.* *(See also **Celebration**.)*

To Gilbert Imlay (extracts)

Paris, August 1793
Past twelve o'clock Monday night

I obey an emotion of my heart, which made me think of wishing thee, my love, good night! before I go to rest, with more tenderness than I can tomorrow, when writing a hasty line or two under Colonel —'s eye. You can scarcely imagine with what pleasure I anticipate the day, when we are to begin almost to live together; and you would smile to hear how many plans of employment I have in my head, now that I am confident my heart has found peace in your bosom. Cherish me with that dignified tenderness, which I have only found in you; and your own dear girl will try to keep under a quickness of feeling, that has sometimes given you pain. Yes, I will be good, that I may deserve to be happy; and whilst you love me, I cannot again fall into the miserable state which rendered life a burthen almost too heavy to be borne.

But, good night! God bless you! Sterne says that is equal to a kiss – yet I would rather give you the kiss into the bargain, glowing with gratitude to Heaven, and affection to you. I like the word affection, because it signifies something habitual; and we are soon to meet, to try whether we have mind enough to keep our hearts warm. I will be at the barrier a little after ten o'clock tomorrow.

Yours

Paris, 1794
Evening, September 23

I have been playing and laughing with the little girl so long, that I cannot take up my pen to address you without emotion. Pressing her to my bosom, she looked so like you (entre nous, your best looks, for I do not admire your commercial face), every nerve seemed to vibrate to the touch, and I began to think that there was something in the assertion of man and wife being one – for you seemed to pervade my whole frame, quickening the beat of my heart, and lending me the sympathetic tears you excited.

Have I anything more to say to you? No; not for the present – the rest is all flown away; and indulging tenderness for you, I cannot now complain of some people here, who have ruffled my temper for two or three days past.

GILLIAN HANSCOMBE (*b.* 1945)
Australia/England

SUNITI NAMJOSHI (*b.* 1941)
India/England

(See also **Declaration**.)

To Suniti Namjoshi

Fragment

. . . so I bowed and nodded as best I could (though not as well as you) and loved the people for loving you and admired the people for admiring you and now and again I sensed you tease or tarry or find something someone said just useful enough to keep and I was (if you'll allow) so proud of you and pleased. . . .

. . . and when we got back to whatever bed we were sharing then, wherever it was, and were undressing ourselves (and each other – it is the same) then one of us said to the other
– well how did we do? sideways, that is? were we all right?
– yes my darling we were all right, said the other;
– but now let us see how we do face to face. . . .

. . . it was always odd (wasn't it?) how there was no afterwards . . . the signs were there: the sweating, the racing of hearts, the heat . . . and we were tired, inevitably . . . but it never actually stopped; there was always a tongue somewhere on an eyebrow or cheek, a hand somewhere, or arms that curved, legs that got muddled; always the climbing or riding or scudding or falling; always the yes saying yes and yes. . . .

. . . and sometimes there was the wondering about who was who. . . .

To Gillian Hanscombe

Be a dolphin then

Be a dolphin then, or be a water woman
and I'll be a dolphin, follow you about,
butt you and nuzzle you, leap into air
and falling back, lie there laughing, while you
my water woman, you'll lie beside me
or lie on me – I'll be your raft. On days
when the wind blows more keenly, we'll cut through
the waves, your thighs gripping me, your nakedness
burning, burning and cooling my back.
But when the sun blazes and penetrates
water, I'll shed my dolphin skin, we'll lie
on the sea floor, our hands on one another's
breasts. Then, as we lie, dive inside me, and surface
splashing; and then, if you like, we'll dive again.

MAUD GONNE (1867–1953)
Ireland

A reappraisal of the life of Maud Gonne is overdue – she has long been seen only as the friend and muse of the poet W.B. Yeats, but her own life was one of political significance, and remarkable commitment and efforts on behalf of the Irish Nationalist cause.

Gonne met Yeats in 1889, when she was twenty-two. It was then, he wrote, 'that the troubling of my life began'. There can be no doubt that Gonne was an attractive, alluring figure, as much for her intelligence, spirit and individuality as for her beauty. Yeats did not know that in 1889 Gonne was already having an affair, and when the child of that affair, Georges, died, she hid the truth from him, telling him that her 'wild sorrow' was because a child she had adopted had died.

Gonne was briefly married and had another child – this relationship ended in a scandalous divorce, adding to her reputation in nineteenth-century Ireland as a 'scarlet woman'. Although the friendship with Yeats lasted forty-five years, she remained ambivalent about sexual involvement with him, succumbing only once. Yeats and Gonne shared a fascination with Irish Celtic mythology, and were active members of the Order of the Golden Dawn. Here she tells Yeats of a strange vision, which heralded what the couple referred to as a 'spiritual marriage' between them. (See also ***Celebration****.)*

To W.B. Yeats

Paris
26 July [1908]

Willie
It is not in a week but in a day that I am writing to you. I had such a wonderful experience last night that I must know at once if it affected you & how? for above all I don't want to do any thing which will take you from your work, or make working more arduous – That play is going to be a wonderful thing & must come first – nothing must interfere with it –

Last night all my household had retired at a quarter to 11 and I thought I would go to you astrally. It was not working hours for you & I thought by going to you I might even be able to leave with you some of my vitality & energy which would make working less of a toil next day – I had seen the day before when waking from sleep a curious some what Egyptian form floating over me (like in the picture of Blake the soul leaving the body) – It was dressed in moth like garments & had curious wings edged with gold in which it could fold itself up – I had thought it was myself, a body in which I could go out into the astral – at a quarter to 11 last night I put on this body & thought strongly of you & desired to go to you. We went some where in space I dont know where – I was conscious of starlight & of hearing the sea below us. You had taken the form I think of a great serpent, but I am not quite sure. I only saw your face distinctly & as I looked into your eyes (as I did the day in Paris you asked me what I was thinking of) & your lips touched mine. We melted into one another till we formed only *one being, a being greater than ourselves* who felt all & knew all with double intensity – the clock striking 11 broke the spell & as we separated it felt as if life was being drawn away from me through my chest with almost physical pain. I went again twice, each time it was the same – each time I was brought back by some slight noise in the house. Then I went upstairs to bed & I dreamed of you confused dreams of ordinary life. We were in Italy together (I think this was from some word in your letter which I had read again before sleeping). We were quite happy, & we talked of this wonderful spiritual vision I have described – you said it would tend to increase physical desire – This troubles me a little – for there was nothing physical in that union – Material union is but a pale shadow compared to it – write to me quickly & tell me if you know anything of this & what you think of it – & if I may come to you again like this. I shall not until I hear from you. My thought with you always.

Maud Gonne

MINNA SIMMONS (1873–1946)
England

The letters and diaries of two working women in the early twentieth century, Ruth Slate and Eva Slawson, have been collected in the book Dear Girl, *edited by Tierl Thompson. Minna Simmons, a warm, uneducated woman, married with four children, formed a late addition to this friendship. Minna and Ruth drew together after the death of Eva, whom they had both loved fiercely.*

Here, Minna confesses her affair with a Mr James (SBJ) to Ruth.

To Ruth

15 July 1916

My Own Beloved,

Never never speak of you disappointing me, do I not love you dear and hold you close to my heart. I hope the time may come when you will need me, so I may prove my love. Are you not Eva's gift to me?

I must be frank and truthful dear to you and so I will tell you what no other eye must ever see. What I now confess is with the deepest shame and humiliation. Yet, dear, with joy, that one can feel as I have felt, is to know the very consciousness of reality. Ruth can you love me after this.

After I had received that letter I showed you and had gone home from my case, *He* [SBJ] came to see me. We had a most lovely talk. We had been to Maude Royden's meeting and it had been the means of one of those soul talks.

Well dear we went into the front room alone and he kissed me, opened my dress and kissed my breasts too, and he said how he felt I was his. He was just going away when he came back and pleaded with me dear to give him everything a woman can give a man. I told him I was sure we should regret it but no dear anything that would make me his. 'Well dear, I did'. The tears I have shed have quite washed away any wrong I did.

My dear Ruth I can never tell you what I suffered. I felt I could never look at anyone again; how I have sat in Church I don't know, it has been simply agony. Well dear I met him out again one evening when I was with Lily and the strangest meeting it seemed, though we never even shook hands. We just mingled together. Then dear he promised to come to Stroud Green to see me, and to write. He did neither. It was simply brutal. Think of me there dear with my tormenting thoughts, my hatred of myself and yet dear I do love him. I knew I was determined it should never happen again.

In my letter I told him there could not be passion between us. If it was to be anything it must be higher than that, told him I knew it couldn't be right or I wouldn't have been so miserable about it. When I asked him if he didn't agree about the latter, he said he had come to the same conclusion.

He said I was more attractive than ever and he simply dare not kiss me or he didn't know what might happen. So dear, I do feel if it has to be anything it must be a pure and noble spiritual bond.

Ruth you do understand dear, all my life I was tied to the tragedy of mated loneliness, if it hadn't been for Eva and Lily and my kiddies I simply couldn't have borne my life. Then to have seemed to have found your mate, and yet dear if I felt he was true and worthy, my life would be a great joy.

I feel we haven't mixed enough with men to know their minds because, dear, he told me he felt like this towards Eva and wished he had given her everything. I can understand him loving you, dear, you are so pretty, but me? Somehow too I feel there is a lot in what he says in his letter. Giving Joan to Eva and Lily has made me see that in Motherhood and Fatherhood the bond is mostly physical and not nearly what has been written about it. You see dear, God showers his gifts on us all and I feel we have only touched the fringe of love.

It will be a hard struggle for us women; men will walk, dear, over our broken and bleeding hearts, but we must love them still in spite of everything.

The strangest thing is, dear, that I haven't felt I wronged Mrs J. No, I felt, dear, what love he gave to me was mine, and never was hers, nor could be. Don't worry about me dear, I have quite regained my self possession.

If he had only written and told me he felt the same and we had blundered, but to be silent and to shun one was bitterly cruel.

I do hope I haven't wearied you. My heart's love dear and my life's devotion.

Your own Minna

VIOLET TREFUSIS (1894–1972)
England

A gifted writer and remarkable figure in her own right, Violet Trefusis is chiefly remembered for her scandalous affair with Vita Sackville-West. After their failed escape from their husbands in 1920, Sackville-West returned to England and her writing; and Trefusis became an expatriate, immersing herself in the international art world.

*Trefusis had an unconventional childhood – her mother, Alice Keppel, was the mistress of King Edward VII – and remained a romantic until her death in Florence in 1972. She began corresponding with Vita Sackville-West in 1910, at the age of sixteen, but Denys Trefusis, her husband, later burned many of the letters between the two women. From those remaining (**see* **Celebration***) it is obvious that although they lived apart, their love for each other never really ended.*

To Vita Sackville-West

Dambatenne, Ceylon
January 2, 1911

I am in a strange mood today, Vita mia, I cannot make up my mind whether I am a freak in every possible respect, or just simply – an unnatural child. Enlighten me by your wisdom and tell me my future, oh pythoness!

I have had every conceivable thing in the way of adventures these last two years. Shall I disclose some of the more thrilling for your benefit? You ask nothing better, do you? And it's exactly because I comprehend your curiosity – quite natural really – that I'm determined not to tell.

I have more memories than if I were a thousand years old. A great chest whose drawers are crammed with balance sheets, verses, love letters, with law suits, novels, with locks of hair rolled up amid the receipts – hides fewer memories than my sad brain. It's a pyramid, an immense vault containing more dead than the common grave. I am a cemetery detested by the moon where, as with remorse, drag out long verses, which fasten themselves to my most sacred deaths.

– *et patati patat*, I could go on reciting for half an hour if this would help to solace my spleen.

Your last missive told me much about your present state. Shall I admit it, not hiding anything, that I've been given much cord to twist again. What a bitch you are! Excuse my language. I employ it on certain occasions *to bury my feelings which are apt to prove too much for me at times.*

Well here's something which I think will make you laugh: imagine, chère amie, that I've brought back an alligator from my jungle expedition – an enormous one such as no longer exists in our times, enormous as the step of a staircase!

This takes your breath away really for once. (I see your scandalised face from here: 'What a vulgar outburst!')

I killed it with my little rifle and if you are very good (as you would say), *you shall have a purse made out of it for your birthday present!*

Do you know that you have ceased to be a reality for me? You are so far away that it seems to me you have never existed outside of my dreams. You are a mirage which recedes to the degree that one approaches to it. Speaking about mirages, I saw a very beautiful one in the Suez Canal at the mouth of the Red Sea. I was gazing with distracted eye at the desert which stretches out to infinity, the intense implacable sun gleaming as a furnace, a camel marching with great unequal steps towards the south – when suddenly I recall letting out a loud cry: 'See over there, the trees, the water?'

One looks: it seems then that a lake encircled by date trees and leafy shrubs, incredibly blue and seductive, had passed unobserved. Immediately we rush to the maps, snatch up the spectacles, then all together to the Captain, who, high up in his cabin is stretched out in a sultry posture. 'What is that lake which glitters in the distance, so blue, so solitary?'

The Captain descends, grumbling, directs his telescope towards the Egyptian shore: 'That, ladies, that is quite simply a mirage!' and he returns to his quarters, still shaking with his habitual healthy and vulgar laughter.

Myself, I remain for a long time leaning on the balustrade with dreaming eyes. I seemed to see so many things in this reality which, after all, was only a mirage.

JANE WELSH CARLYLE (1801–66)
England

Heiress Jane Welsh was known as 'The Flower of Haddington'. After more than thirty letters of entreaty, she agreed to marry Thomas Carlyle in 1826. It seems that her earlier protestations – that she loved him, but was not in love *with him – proved true. After her death from an accident in 1866, Carlyle was saddened to discover from his wife's diaries that – contrary to her feelings at the time of the following letter of acceptance – she had been unhappy in the marriage.* *(See also* ***Rejection*** *.)*

To Thomas Carlyle

Templand,
Tuesday 3rd Oct 1826

Oh, my dearest Friend! be always *so* good to me, and I shall make the best and happiest Wife. When I read in your looks and words that you love me, I feel it in the deepest part of my soul; then I care not one jot for the whole Universe beside; but when you fly from my caresses to – smoke tobacco, or speak of me as a new *circumstance* of your lot, then indeed my 'heart is troubled about many things.'

My Mother is not come yet, but is expected this week; the week following must be given to her to take a last look at her Child; and then Dearest, God willing, I am your own for ever and ever. . . .

Oh mercy! What I would give to be sitting in our doll's house married for a week! . . . [And referring to his sister Jane coming to stay with them] . . . and give her a kiss in my name.

I may well return *one* out of *twenty*. But indeed, Dear, these kisses on paper are scarce worth keeping. You gave me one on my neck that night you were in such good-humour, and one on my lips on some forgotten occasion, that I would not part with for a hundred thousand paper ones. Perhaps some day or other, I shall get none of either sort; *sic transit gloria mundi* ['so passes the glory of the world'] . . . And then not my will be done, but thine. I am going to be really a very meek-tempered Wife; indeed, I am begun to be meek-tempered already. My Aunt tells me, she could live for ever with *me*, without quarrelling – I am so reasonable and equal in my humour. There is something to gladden your heart withal! and more than this; my Grandfather observed while I was supping my porridge last night, that 'she was really a douce peaceable body that *Pen*.' So you perceive, my good Sir, the fault will be wholly your own, if we do not get on most harmoniously together. . . . But I must stop. And this is my last Letter. What a thought! How terrible and yet full of bliss. You will love me for ever, will you not, my own Husband? and I will always be your true and affectionate

Jane Welsh

REJECTION:
'Let it be friendship meanwhile'

JANE WELSH CARLYLE (1801–66)
England

(See also **Consummation**.)

To Thomas Carlyle

Seaforth, Tuesday, July 14, 1846

Oh! my dear Husband, Fortune has played me such a cruel trick this day! But it is all right now; and I do not even feel any resentment against Fortune for the suffocating misery of the last two hours. I know always, even when I seem to you most exacting, that whatever happens to me is nothing like so bad as I deserve. But you shall hear all how it was.

. . . Not a line from you on my Birthday – on the fifth day! I did not burst out crying – did not faint – did not *do* anything absurd, so far as I know, but I walked back again, without speaking a word; and with such a tumult of wretchedness in my heart as you who know me can conceive. And then I shut myself in my own room to fancy everything that was most tormenting. Were you, finally, so out of patience with me that you had resolved to write to me no more at all? Had you gone to Addiscombe, and found no leisure there to remember my existence? Were you taken ill, so ill that you *could* not write? That last idea made me mad to get off to the railway, and back to London. Oh, mercy! what a two hours I had of it! And just when I was at my wit's end, I heard Julia crying out thro' the house: 'Mrs Carlyle, Mrs Carlyle! are you there? Here is a letter for you!' And so there was after all! The post-mistress had overlooked it, and given it to Robert, when he went afterwards, not knowing that we had been. I wonder what *Love-letter* was ever received with such thankfulness! Oh, my Dear! I am not fit for living in the world with this organisation. I am as much broken to pieces by that little accident as if I had come thro' an attack of cholera or typhus fever. I cannot even steady my hand to *write* decently. But I felt an irresistible need of thanking you, by return of post. Yes, I have kissed the dear little Card-case; and now I will lie down a while, and try to get some sleep, at least to quieten myself. I will try to believe – oh, why cannot I believe it, once for all – that, with all my faults and follies, I *am* 'dearer to you than any earthly creature!' I will be better for Geraldine here; she is become very quiet and nice, and as affectionate for me as ever.

Your own

Jane Carlyle

ANNE GUDIS (*b.* 1923)
USA

(See also Anne Gudis's letter to Samuel Kramer in **Invitation**.)

Newark, Sept. 7, 1943

Mr Kramer:
Go To Hell!
With love,
Anne Gudis

Anne Gudis found herself the subject of much unfavourable attention after the publication of this letter in Yank *magazine. Kramer's commanding officer wrote to her, advising her that her words were affecting war morale. In December, she wrote again.*

To Samuel Kramer (extract)

Newark, Dec. [?], 1943

Mr Kramer,
This letter is going to be brutally frank and I'm not going to spare any words. It is not my nature to use them, but if I do it's entirely your fault. I only hope this letter leaves you feeling the way I did after reading your last two letters.

After reading the one I received last month, I decided to hell with him, he isn't worth the time, or effort it takes to write to him.

You're so damn conceited you think that if a girl so much as looks at you she wants to marry you, and the same with my letter writing. I thought that something could come of it, but after these few incidents at Penn Station, I lost all romantic interest in you. How could I hold on or be in love with you, when you take into consideration the circumstances of the whole incident. Please understand I have no marital interests in you whatsoever.

I wrote to you as a friend and thought my letters would be appreciated but since they annoy you so, I shall stop my so called folly.

Don't tell me what to do either. You nor anyone else will dictate my life for me. Taking that course in psychoanalysis has helped me understand why you are so very heartless. Of course it's not your fault that you should forgive and forget, but because you don't you deserve whatever you get. I have to laugh, you once wrote and told me to have compassion, well why don't you practice what you preach, you inebriate and don't tell me to get married either.

When I get married, it's not just to sleep with a man, because I can find plenty of bed mates, without being married, and remember for the past 10 months, I haven't even had a date or kissed a fellow. Perhaps I am not normal, that's why. And I don't want to marry the type of man you represent. But, damn it, you men are all alike.

Anne

ANNE BOLEYN (1502/7–36)
England

Anne Boleyn was secretly married to King Henry VIII in 1533. She was his second wife. Three years later, when she playfully tossed her handkerchief at the feet of an admirer in court, the King found the excuse he was looking for to get rid of her. She was charged with and found guilty of high treason. One of those she was accused of committing adultery with was her own brother. They were both beheaded a few days later.

The following letter, beseeching Henry to see reason, was written while Boleyn was imprisoned in the Tower. Doubts have been voiced as to the letter's authenticity – but if it is a fake, it is a skilled fake, eloquently expressing 'the expostulations of a slighted lover, the resentments of an injured woman, and the sorrows of an imprisoned queen'.

To Henry VIII

(1536)

Sir, – Your Grace's displeasure, and my imprisonment, are things so strange unto me, as what to write, or what to excuse, I am altogether ignorant. Whereas you send unto me (willing me to confess a truth, and so obtain your favour) by such an one, whom you know to be mine ancient professed enemy, I no sooner received this message by him, than I rightly conceived your meaning; and if, as you say, confessing a truth indeed may procure my safety, I shall with all willingness and duty perform your command.

But let not your Grace ever imagine that your poor wife will ever be brought to acknowledge a fault, where not so much as a thought thereof preceded. And to speak a truth, never Prince had wife more loyal in all duty, and in all true affection, than you have ever found in Anne Boleyn; with which name and place I could willingly have contented myself, if God and your Grace's pleasure had been so pleased. Neither did I at any time so far forget myself in my exaltation or received Queenship, but that I always looked for such an alteration as I now find; for the ground of my preferment being on no surer foundation than your Grace's fancy, the least alteration, I knew, was fit and sufficient to draw that fancy to some other object. You have chosen me, from a low estate, to be your queen and companion, far beyond my desert or desire. If then, you find me worthy of such honour, good your Grace, let not any light fancy, or bad counsel of mine enemies, withdraw your princely favour from me; neither let that stain, that unworthy stain, of a disloyal heart towards your good Grace, ever cast so foul a blot on your most dutiful wife, and the Infant-Princess your daughter. Try me, good King, but let me have a lawful trial, and let not my sworn enemies sit as my accusers and judges; yea, let me receive an open trial, for my truth shall fear no open shame. Then shall you see either mine innocence cleared, your suspicion and conscience satisfied, the ignominy and slander of the world stopped, or my guilt openly declared. . . .

But if you have already determined of me, and that not only my death, but an infamous slander must bring you the enjoying of your desired happiness; then I desire of God, that He will pardon your great sin therein, and likewise mine enemies, the instruments thereof, and that He will not call you to a strict account for your unprincely and cruel usage of me, at his general judgment-seat, where both you and myself must shortly appear, and in whose judgment I doubt not (whatsoever the world may think of me) mine innocence shall be openly and sufficiently cleared.

My last and only request shall be that myself may only bear the burden of your Grace's displeasure, and that it may not touch the innocent souls of those poor gentlemen who (as I understand) are likewise in strait imprisonment for my sake. If ever I have found favour in your sight, if ever the name of Anne Boleyn hath been pleasing in your ears, then let me obtain this request, and I will so leave to trouble your Grace any further, with mine earnest prayers to the Trinity to have your Grace in His good keeping, and to direct you in all your actions. From my doleful prison in the Tower, this sixth of May.

Your most loyal and ever faithful wife,

Anne Boleyn

QUEEN ELIZABETH I (1533–1603)
England

Elizabeth I was the daughter of Anne Boleyn and King Henry VIII. Lord Admiral Seymour proposed to her shortly after the death of her father, in 1547, when she was about to become Queen of England. Here she replies.

To Lord Admiral Seymour

February 27, 1547

My Lord Admiral, – The letter you have written to me is the most obliging, and, at the same time, the most eloquent in the world. And as I do not feel myself competent to reply to so many courteous expressions, I shall content myself with unfolding to you, in few words, my real sentiments. I confess to you that your letter, all eloquent as it is, has very much surprised me; for, besides that neither my age nor my inclination allows me to think of marriage, I never could have believed that any one would have spoken to me of nuptials at a time when I ought to think of nothing but sorrow for the death of my father. And to him I owe so much, that I must have two years at least to mourn for his loss. And how can I make up my mind to become a wife before I shall have enjoyed for some years my virgin state, and arrived at years of discretion?

Permit me, then, my Lord Admiral, to tell you frankly, that as there is no one in the world who more esteems your merit than myself, or who sees you with more pleasure as a disinterested person, so would I preserve to myself the privilege of recognising you as such, without entering into that strict bond of matrimony, which often causes one to forget the possession of true merit. Let your highness be well persuaded that though I decline the happiness of becoming your wife I shall never cease to interest myself in all that can crown your merit with glory, and shall ever feel the greatest pleasure in being your servant and good friend.

Elizabeth

ROSA FERRUCCI (1835–57)
Italy

Rosa Ferrucci was an Italian writer and mystic. Her mother was a poet, the translator into English of Ferrucci's letters to Gaetano, who courted her devotedly for a year in 1856.

There is much hesitation in Ferrucci's rejection of Gaetano's advances. She sounds frail and confused. She died a year later, before the projected marriage could take place.

To Gaetano

Pisa, 23 June 1856

I thank you for your kind intention to come to Pisa on Wednesday. Although my birthday is always a solemn and joyous event, yet this year I shall regard it as more sacred than ever, being under a sense of deeper gratitude to God, and feeling that I must thank him for all the favours which he has heaped on me all my life and particularly of late. . . .

I am not ready to marry you at once, because, however much I love you, I do not wish to experience now the pain that will surely be mine when I leave my parental home.

I would be willing to make it eleven months instead of fifteen and I assure you that this would be a real proof of affection, for the sacrifice of four months of intimate life with the most affectionate of mothers is a supreme one; nevertheless, I am willing to make it for your sake.

Rosa

15 Sept. 1856

Just as yesterday I was full of joy, so today I am sad. Your being far away, the thought of my inevitable separation from mama and the child, all this has caused me to become despondent and to weep.

Poor women. We are frailer than the leaves, which every impetuous gust of wind disturbs and scatters; and when the youth of our poor hearts, which know but to love, and suffer, is finished, we are divided between a thousand thoughts, pleasant and sad. But forgive me, oh God, for I should not be sad, but should thank thee.

I open my mind to you, my Gaetano, for you must be the comfort and guidance of my future life, you must divine every thought, disperse all my vain fears, advise and aid me always. I will not conceal from you that my future state has quickened my affections so that, thinking of it, I become alternately sad and happy, as never before. But what would you? I do not know at all how I shall be able to tear myself from the arms of her who has reared me with such care and loved me so dearly. But enough for today. I cannot speak of mama any more because my eyes are full of tears. I cannot understand myself. I wish to curb my sensibility and then my heart overpowers my reason.

Dear, October is approaching. If then I shall be unable to enjoy the country holiday myself, I shall nevertheless think with pleasure of the delight it will afford you. You will see your mountains again, and the pine-woods which I have gazed on since childhood with such rapture, and surrounded by the flowers, the grass and the beautiful trees, you will be turned in thought to the Creator of all; you will admire and love the wonderful creations of the Power which has this year revealed to you a new life, which I fervently hope will be free from tribulation. Oh, how much the love of God grows in us when we contemplate the marvels of nature! How we ought always to prove by our actions and thoughts our deepest sense of gratitude to God, in whom our lives should be wholly bound up. He who is so bountiful gives not only the dew and the rain to the parched fields, the leaves to the trees, flowers to the meadow, but vouchsafes us solace in every affliction because in him our nature reposes.

I have spoken of God because I feel that thinking of him gives such comfort and aid to our lives.

Ever thine,

Rosa

FREYA STARK (1893–1993)
Europe

The famous traveller Freya Stark journeyed all her life in rough or exotic places, developing a taste for travel adventures at the age of four, embarking on trips on her own through Persia or the Near East when no European woman had done so before. She was also a gifted and conscientious letter writer.

Relationships had to be squeezed in between trips, but she managed several. In her fifties she made the decision – surprising even to herself – to marry Stewart Perowne, and in the first of these letters she breaks the news to her long-standing friend Nigel Clive. Elsewhere Stark says of married life: 'Even a misanthropist would say that marriage gives one the advantage of having someone to get away from occasionally and increases one's capacity to suffer.'

The second letter is to her husband Perowne, four years later.

To Nigel Clive

Asolo. 14 September 1947

My dearest Nigel,

Such a peculiar thing has happened: I have promised to marry Stewart. I have not written to anyone to tell them yet; but I must say so at once to you, for you are very dear to me, nor do I feel that this or anything else will affect it. I hope you will feel this too, and make me happy by saying so. If you had been old, or I young, we might have lived our lives together; or perhaps we might not have cared for each other or not realised it. As it is, we hold hands across a river of time. Nigel darling, please remain my dearest of friends.

It is one of the happy things that Stewart likes the people I like. We have a common world to set out in. He is being sent to Antigua. I believe he just couldn't bear to go alone and had to have a wife among his tropical kit. Anyway, I am by way of going out in a few months, and going now to London to see it all through in a deplorable hurry. So it all seems very unreal at the moment. I think, too, it will mean no Greece in January, and I don't mind in the least if you are not to be there. But you *must* come here when next I am back, probably in the summer.

Don't mention anything till you see it officially announced.

Dear love,

Freya

To Stewart Perowne

Asolo. 19 March 1951

My darling,

Things are so sad and superficial between us that I have long been feeling that they cannot go on as they were and have only waited to write or speak because I could not bear you to think that any trivial cause, or want of affection, made me do it; and also because I hoped that you yourself might feel this thing so near your heart as to make you speak before I left.

I don't know whose the fault, anyway it doesn't matter. If it were just that the thing has failed, it would be simple. We are both independent, and we could separate and go back to where we were. I do care for you, but I have tried to take myself out of this account and to think of the whole thing without any bias as far as I can; one of these days I believe you will discover that you do care.

Let it be friendship meanwhile, and not just acquaintance. Half a dozen people around us tell me their hearts more intimately than you do. Better just to come and go as friends and that I will always be. There is nothing but true affection in my heart.

I have kept this for a day before sending, feeling perhaps that I might not send it at all, but there *must* be a truth between us, and it is the truth. Let it not make any difference to what we are to each other, such dear friends, and with true and safe affection, let it only take away what there was of pretence. I long for you to come here and you know it is your true home.

Love,

Freya

ANNE ISABELLA BYRON (1792–1860)
England

A vast literature has grown up debating the reasons for the breakdown of the brief marriage of the poet Lord Byron to Lady Anne Isabella. This seems surprising in the light of the evidence available to us; here Lady Byron herself gives some pretty straightforward indications of her dissatisfaction.

To Lord Byron

Kirkby, Feb. 13, 1816

On reconsidering your last letter to me, and your second to my father, I find some allusions which I will not leave to be answered by others because the explanation may be less disagreeable to you from myself.

My letters of January 15th and 16th. It can be fully and clearly proved that I left your house under the persuasion of your having a complaint of so dangerous a nature that any agitation might bring on a fatal crisis. My entreaties before I quitted you that you would take medical advice, repeated in my letter of January 15th, must convince you of such an impression on my mind. My absence, if it had not been rendered necessary by other causes, was medically recommended on that ground, as removing an object of irritation. I should have acted inconsistently with my unchanged affection for you, or indeed with the common principles of humanity, by urging my wrongs at that moment. From subsequent accounts I found that these particular apprehensions which I, and others, had entertained, were groundless. Till they were ascertained to be so, it was my intention to induce you to come to this place where, at every hazard, I would have devoted myself to the alleviation of *your* sufferings, and should not then have reminded you of *my own*, as believing you, from physical causes, not to be *accountable* for them. My parents, under the same impression communicated to me, felt the kindest anxiety to promote my wishes and your recovery, by receiving you here. Of all this my letter of January 16th is a testimony. If for these reasons (to which others were perhaps added) I did not remonstrate at the time of leaving your house, you cannot forget that I had before warned you, earnestly and affectionately, of the unhappy and irreparable consequences which must ensure from your conduct, both to yourself and to me, that to those representations you had replied by a determination to be wicked, though it should break my heart.

What then had I to expect? I cannot attribute your 'state of mind' to any cause so much as the *total* dereliction of principle, which, since our marriage, you have professed and gloried in. Your acknowledgments have not been accompanied by any intentions of amendment.

I have consistently fulfilled my duty as your wife. It was too dear to be resigned till it became hopeless. Now my resolution cannot be changed.

A.I. Byron

VIOLET COWARD (20th Century)
England

The mother of playwright Noël Coward, here writing to her husband Arthur.

To Arthur Coward

Dear Arthur,
This letter will probably come as a shock to you, I have made friends so often and it has taken a long time to kill my affection for you, but you have at last succeeded in doing so. . . . As long as I can remember, not once have you ever stood up for me or the boys when we have been in any little trouble, you have *always* taken the opposite side and been against us. I remember so many times when you have failed me: and this has been the last straw. How *dare* you behave as you have been doing lately. I have never been so miserable in my life since I came from Ceylon, and who are you to dare to make my life so unhappy. What have you ever done for me or for either of your fine boys to help them on in life. You have never done anything to help anybody, and everything has been done for you. And yet you are so far from being ashamed of yourself that you plump yourself down on us, full of conceit, selfishness and self

appreciation and spoil our lives for us. No one with any pretensions to being a gentleman could ever bully any woman as you bully my sister. It is *shameful* in front of those children too. [Presumably Noël and Erik.] She has as great a right to be here as you have. Noël chose to give her a home before he gave you one, and why are you not earning your living? You are strong and healthy and will no doubt live to be 100, a burden on Noël, not to speak of putting your wife on him too. Now I have come to a decision. I am going to add still more to poor Noël's burden and ask him to provide you with another home. If he agrees I will find you a cottage somewhere, with a little less grandeur than you have here which will do you good. Noël has always understood your character and what I have been through, and will do anything he can to make me happy again. For the present things must remain as they are and I must put up with you, but in a different way. I shall never stand up for you again as I have always done, and I tell you definitely, everything is over between you and me. The last scrap of my affection for you has gone and it is entirely your own fault.

Violet

CHARLOTTE CARPENTER (1777–?)
France/England

Charlotte Carpenter was engaged to the writer Walter Scott. Of French descent, an orphan, as she explains in her letter, Carpenter had been adopted by Lord Downshire and taken to live in the Lake District, where she met Scott.

Even at this early stage in their relationship Carpenter is attuned to Scott's attempts to dominate her, and gently rebukes him – 'it is beginning rather too soon'.

To Walter Scott

(Oct. 1797)

Indeed, Mr Scott, I am by no means pleased with all this writing. I have told you how much I dislike it, and yet you still persist in asking me to write, and that by return of post.

O! you are really quite out of your senses. I should not have indulged you in that whim of yours, had you not given me that hint that my silence gives an air of mystery. I have no reason that can detain me in acquainting you that my father and my mother were French, of the name of Charpentier; he had a place under Government; their residence was at Lyons, where you would find on inquiries that they lived in good repute and in *very good style.* I had the misfortune of losing my father before I could know the value of such a parent. At his death we were left to the care of Lord D[ownshire], who was his very great friend; and very soon after, I had the affliction of losing my mother. Our taking the name of Carpenter was on my brother's going to India, to prevent any difficulties that might have occurred. I hope now you are pleased. Lord D[ownshire] could have given you every information, as he has been acquainted with all my family.

You say you almost love *him*; but until your *almost* comes to a *quite*, I cannot love *you.*

Before I conclude this famous epistle, I will give you a little hint – that is, not to put so many *musts* in your letters – it is beginning *rather too soon*; and another thing is, that I take the liberty not to mind them much, but I expect you [? to] mind me.

You *must* take care of yourself, you *must* think of me and believe me.

Yours sincerely,

C.C.

MRS HOWARD
(Late 17th/Early 18th Century)
England

'Mrs Howard', later Countess of Suffolk and mistress of George II, was a vivacious socialite who drew many admirers; among them Charles Mordaunt, Lord Peterborough. The poet John Gay is said to have helped her with her letters to Lord Peterborough. Whether Gay's words or her own, they have a surprisingly modern ring; that women wish to be considered as neither devils nor angels, but merely women.

To Lord Peterborough

172–?

I have carefully perused your lordship's letter about your fair devil and your black devil, your hell and tortures, your heaven and happiness – those sublime expressions which ladies and gentlemen use in their gallantries and distresses.

I suppose by your fair devil you mean nothing less than an angel. If so, my lord, I beg leave to give some reasons why I think a woman is neither like an angel nor a devil, and why successful and unhappy love do not in the least resemble heaven and hell. It is true, you may quote these thousand gallant letters and precedents for the use of these love terms, which have a mighty captivating sound in the ears of a woman, and have been with equal propriety applied to all women in all ages.

In the first place, my lord, an angel pretends to be nothing else but a *spirit*. If, then, a woman was no more than an angel what could a lover get by the pursuit?

The black devil is a spirit too, but one that has lost her beauty and retained her pride. Tell a woman this and ask how she likes the simile.

The pleasure of an angel is offering praise; the pleasure of a woman is receiving it.

Successful love is very unlike heaven, because you may have success one hour, and lose it the next. Heaven is unchangeable. Who can say so of love letters? In love there are as many heavens as there are women; so that, if a man be so unhappy as to lose one heaven, he need not throw himself headlong into hell.

This thought might be carried further. But perhaps you will ask me, if a woman be neither like angel or devil, what is she like? I answer, that the only thing that is like a woman is – *another woman.*

How often has your lordship persuaded foreign ladies that nothing but them could make you forsake your dear country? But at present I find it is more to your purpose to tell me that I am the only woman that could prevail with you to stay in your ungrateful country.

'VANESSA' [ESTHER VANHOMRIGH] (1690–1723)
Holland/England

'Vanessa' was of Dutch descent, living in London with her mother, a rich widow, when in 1710 she met the Irish writer Jonathan Swift. She developed an infatuation with him. On his return to Ireland Swift corresponded with Vanessa, inflaming her 'violent passion' for him. When rumours reached her of Swift's intended marriage to another, Vanessa wrote begging for confirmation. In fury, Swift travelled to her home, flung the letter back at her and left. Vanessa is said to have died from the shock.

In the following two letters to Swift, written in the early stages of their correspondence, Vanessa admonishes him for his failure to write.

To Jonathan Swift

You bid me be easy, and you would see me as often as you could. You had better have said, as often as you could get the better of your inclinations so much, or as often as you remember there was such a one in the world. If you continue to treat me as you do, you will not be made uneasy by me long. It is impossible to describe what I have suffered since I saw you last. I am sure I could have borne the rack much better than those killing, killing words of yours. Sometimes I have resolved to die without seeing you more, but those resolves, to your misfortune, did not last long. For there is something in human nature that prompts one so to find relief in this world, I must give way to it, and beg you would see me, and speak kindly to me; for I am sure you would not condemn any one to suffer what I have done, could you but know it. The reason I write to you is, because I cannot tell it to you should I see you; for when I begin to complain, then you are angry, and there is something in your looks so awful, that it strikes me dumb. O! but that you may have but so much regard for me left, that this complaint may touch your soul with pity! I say as little as ever I can; did you but know what I thought, I am sure it would move you to forgive me: and believe I cannot help telling you this and live.

London, September 1, 1712

Had I a correspondent in China, I might have had an answer by this time. I never could think till now that London was so far off in your thoughts, and that twenty miles were, by your computation, equal to some thousands. I thought it a piece of charity to undeceive you in this point, and to let you know, if you give yourself the trouble to write, I may probably receive your letter in a day: 'twas that made me venture to take pen in hand the third time. Sure you'll not let it be to no purpose. . . .

E. Vanhomrigh

GEORGE SAND (1804–76)
France

*See also George Sand's letter (in **Invitation**) to her doctor, Pagello, written while her lover, the poet Alfred de Musset, was ill. Sand's fling with Pagello brought about the end of the Sand–de Musset liaison, but it is clear from the following (written afterwards, in some regret) that she felt deeply for de Musset.*

To Alfred de Musset (extract)

15–17 April 1834

Never, never believe, Alfred, that I could be happy if I thought I had lost your heart. Whether I have been mistress or mother to you, what does that matter? Whether I have inspired you by love or by friendship, whether I have been happy or unhappy with you – nothing of this affects the present state of my mind. I know that I love you, that is all. . . . To watch over you, to keep you from all harm, from all friction; to surround you with distractions and pleasures, that is the need which awakens regret in me since I lost you. Why has a task so sweet, a task which I should have undertaken so joyfully, become little by little so bitter, and then suddenly impossible? What fate has intervened to turn my remedies into poisons? How is it that I, who would have given all my vitality to give you a night's repose and peace, have become a torment, a scourge, a spectre to you? When these atrocious memories besiege me (and at what hour do they leave me in peace?), I go nearly mad, I soak my pillow with tears; I hear in the silence of the night your voice calling me. Who will call me now? Who will need me to keep watch? How am I to use up the strength which I had accumulated for you and which now turns against me? Oh, my child, my child! How much I need your tenderness and your forgiveness! Never ask me for mine, and never say you have wronged me: how did I know? I remember nothing except that we have been very unhappy and have parted; but I know, I feel, that all our lives we shall love one another from our heart, from our intelligence, and that we shall by a holy affection try to cure ourselves mutually of the ills that we have each suffered for the other.

Alas, no! we were not to blame; we obeyed our destiny, for our natures, more impulsive than others', prevented us living the life of ordinary lovers; but we were born to know and to love each other, be sure of that. Had it not been for your youth and the weakness which your tears produced in me one morning, we should have remained brother and sister. . . .

You were right, our embraces were an incest, but we knew it not; we threw ourselves innocently and sincerely into each other's arms. Well now, have those embraces left us a single remembrance which is not chaste and holy? On a day of fever and delirium you reproached me with never having made you feel the pleasures of love. I shed tears at that, but now I am well content that there should have been something true in that speech. I am well content that those pleasures have been more austere, more veiled than any you will find elsewhere. At least you, in the arms of other women, will not be reminded of me. But when you are alone, when you feel the need to pray and to shed tears, you will think of your George, of your true comrade, of your sick-nurse, of your friend, of something better than that. For the sentiment which unites us is combined of so many things, that it can compare to none other. The world will never understand it at all; so much the better. We love each other and we can snap our fingers at it.

Goodbye, goodbye, my dearest little one. Write me very often, I beg of you. Oh that I knew you arrived safe and sound in Paris! Remember that you have promised to take care of yourself. Goodbye, my Alfred, love your George. Send me, I beg, twelve pairs of glacé gloves, six yellow and six of colour. Send me, above all, the verses you have made. All, I have not a single one!

Translated by Félix Decori

DESOLATION:
'My heart is broke'

VITA SACKVILLE-WEST (1892–1962)
England

Novelist, poet and biographer. Author of, amongst others, Knole and the Sackvilles *(1922),* Heritage *(a novel, 1922),* The Land *(long poem, 1927) and* All Passion Spent *(her most commercially successful novel, 1931).*

In 1914 she married Harold Nicolson, and while initially she accompanied him when he was posted overseas, eventually she chose to remain in England. Vita Sackville-West fell in love with Violet Trefusis in 1918, beginning a torrid affair with her, at the same time as she began her famous, enduring friendship with Virginia Woolf. Despite Sackville-West's affairs and Nicolson's own homosexuality, the marriage survived and is described by their son Nigel Nicolson in Portrait of a Marriage *(1973). (See also letters in* ***Invitation****,* ***Declaration****,* ***Consummation*** *and* ***Celebration****.)*

To Virginia Woolf

Milan [posted in Trieste]
Thursday 21 [January] 1926

I am reduced to a thing that wants Virginia. I composed a beautiful letter to you in the sleepless nightmare hours of the night, and it has all gone: I just miss you, in a quite simple desperate human way. You, with all your un-dumb letters, would never write so elementary a phrase as that; perhaps you wouldn't even feel it. And yet I believe you'll be sensible of a little gap. But you'd clothe it in so exquisite a phrase that it would lose a little of its reality. Whereas with me it is quite stark: I miss you even more than I could have believed; and I was prepared to miss you a good deal. So this letter is just really a squeal of pain. It is incredible how essential to me you have become. I suppose you are accustomed to people saying these things. Damn you, spoilt creature; I shan't make you love me any the more by giving myself away like this – But oh my dear, I *can't* be clever and stand-offish with you: I love you too much for that. Too truly. You have no idea how stand-offish I can be with people I don't love. I have brought it to a fine art. But you have broken down my defences. And I don't really resent it.

However I won't bore you with any more.

We have re-started, and the train is shaky again. I shall have to write at the stations – which are fortunately many across the Lombard plain.

Venice. The stations were many, but I didn't bargain for the Orient

Express not stopping at them. And here we are at Venice for ten minutes only, – a wretched time in which to try and write. No time to buy an Italian stamp even, so this will have to go from Trieste.

The waterfalls in Switzerland were frozen into solid iridescent curtains of ice, hanging over the rock; so lovely. And Italy all blanketed in snow.

We're going to start again. I shall have to wait till Trieste tomorrow morning. Please forgive me for writing such a miserable letter.

V.

A year later

Near Hanover
Saturday 29 [January]

My darling
I hoped I should wake up less depressed this morning, but I didn't. I went to bed last night as black as a sweep. The awful dreariness of Westphalia makes it worse: factory towns, mounds of slag, flat country, and some patches of dirty snow. And you are going to the Webbs. Well, well. . . .

Why aren't you with me? Oh, why? I do want you so frightfully.

The only thing which gives me any pleasure is Leigh's get-up. He has bought a short sheepskin coat, in which he evidently thinks he looks like a Hungarian shepherd, but horn-rimmed glasses and a rather loud pair of plus-fours destroy this effect. Dottie on the other hand has appeared in a very long fur-coat, down to the ankles, so thick as to make her quite round; *she* looks like a Russian grand-duke. We are all rather cross, and have rows about luggage. I want more than ever to travel with you; it seems to me now the height of my desire, and I get into despair wondering how it can ever be realised. Can it, do you think? Oh my lovely Virginia, it is dreadful how I miss you, and everything that everybody says seems flat and stupid.

I do hope more and more that you won't go to America, I am sure it would be too tiring for you, and anyway I am sure you wouldn't like it. Come to Beirut instead??

So we bundle along over Germany, and very dull it is – Surely I haven't lost my zest for travel? no, it is not that; it is simply that I want to be with you and not with anybody else – But you will get bored if I go on saying this, only it comes back and back till it drips off my pen – Do you realise that I shall have to wait for over a fortnight before I can hear from you? poor me. I hadn't thought of that before leaving, but now it bulks very large and horrible. What may not happen to you in the course of a fortnight? you may get ill, fall in love, Heaven knows what.

I shall work so hard, partly to please you, partly to please myself, partly to make the time go and have something to show for it. I treasure your sudden discourse on literature yesterday morning, – a send-off to me, rather like Polonius to Laertes. It is quite true that you have had infinitely more influence on me intellectually than anyone, and for this alone I love you. I feel my muscles hardening,

> *'Il poeta è un' artiere*
> *Che al mestiere*
> *Fece i muscoli d'acciaio. . . .'*

Yes, my very dear Virginia, I was at a crossways just about the time I first met you.

You do like me to write well, don't you? And I do hate writing badly – and having written so badly in the past. But now, like Queen Victoria, I will be good.

Hell! I wish you were here – The team of ponies prances with temper. Send me anything you write in papers, and send 'On reading'. Please. I hope you will get my letters quick and often. Tell me if I write too often. I love you.

V.

MARIANA ALCOFORADO (17th Century)
Portugal

Love Letters of a Portuguese Nun, *supposedly written between 1667 and 1668 by Soror Mariana Alcoforado to her soldier lover Noël Bouton, while she was cloistered in a convent in Beja, caused a furore when it was first translated and published in France in 1669. The work has since been exposed as a possible forgery (the real author being the translator of the letters, Guilleragues). Alcoforado's searing lyric passion in the face of desertion by her lover, and the story of the twenty-five-year-old virgin who gives herself to a dazzling suitor, only to suffer abandonment, has many times been the inspiration for other works of literature.*

Fourth letter of a Portuguese Nun

It seems to me that I am doing the greatest possible wrong to the feelings of my heart in trying to make them clear in writing to you. How happy I should be if you could guess them by the violence of your own! But I cannot depend upon you, and I cannot keep myself from telling you – although much less bitterly than I feel it – that you ought not ill-treat me, as you do, with a neglect that is driving me to despair and even brings shame upon yourself. It is fitting at least that you permit me to complain of the woes which I foresaw when I found that you were determined to leave me. I deceived myself – it is so clear now – when I expected you to act in better faith than is usual in these situations; for the depth of my love seemed to lift me above any sort of suspicion, and to call for more than the usual degree of faithfulness on your part. But your inclination to betray me is so great that it overpowers the gratitude you owe for all I have done for you. Of course I should not cease to be very unhappy if you loved me only because I loved you – I should prefer to owe everything to your affection alone – but even this is so far from being the case that I have not received a single letter from you in six months! I attribute all this misfortune to the blindness with which I entered into this attachment. Should I not have foreseen that my happiness was bound to come to an end sooner than my love? Could I hope that you would spend all your life in Portugal, that you would renounce your country and your fortune to think only of me? My pain is without solace, and the remembrance of past pleasures overwhelms me with despair. Can all my longing really be in vain? Shall I never see you here in my room again, ardent and passionate as you once were?

But alas! I must not deceive myself again; I know only too well that the emotions which filled my mind and heart to the exclusion of everything else were for you only the products of fleeting desire, coming and going with the pleasure of the moment. In those too happy moments I should have called reason to my aid to moderate the fatal excess of my delight, to give me some hint of my present suffering. But I gave myself to you entirely – I was in no state to give thought to anything which might poison my happiness or prevent me from enjoying to the full the ardent proofs of your passion. I was too blissfully conscious of your nearness to think that someday you might be gone from me. I remember, however, that sometimes I did say that you would make me miserable . . . but these fears were soon dissipated, and I took pleasure in offering them to you as a sacrifice, in giving myself up to the enchantment and deceit of your protestations. The remedy for all my ills I see very plainly – if I no longer loved you, I should be free of them. But what remedy is that! No, I would suffer even more rather than forget you. But alas! does this depend upon me? I cannot reproach myself with having wished even for a single moment not to go on loving you. You are more to be pitied than I. It is better to bear all that I am suffering than to wallow in the languid pleasures that your mistresses in France may give you. I do not envy your indifference . . . in fact, I pity you. I defy you to forget me utterly; I flatter myself that I have brought you to such a point that your pleasures must be imperfect without me; and I am much happier than you because I am much busier.

Recently they made me portress of the convent. Every one who speaks to me thinks I am mad – I do not know what answers I give them, and the nuns must be as crazy as I to think me capable of taking care of anything.

Oh how I envy the happiness of Francisco and Manuel! Why am I not always with you as they are? I should have followed you and served you with more zeal. My only wish in this world is to see you. At least, remember me! I could content myself with your remembering me, but I dare not be sure even of that. When I saw you every day I did not limit my hopes to this, but you have made me understand that I must submit to your will in everything. And yet I do not regret having adored you . . . I am even glad to have been betrayed by you. All the harshness of your absence – eternal though it may prove to be – in no way diminishes the strength of my love. I want the whole world to know of it. I make no secret of it, and I am delighted to have done all that I did for you alone and in defiance of all propriety. It was my honour, my religion, to love you desperately for the rest of my life once I had begun to love you.

I do not say all this to make you feel obliged to write to me. Feel no compulsion. I wish nothing of you that does not come of your own free will . . . I renounce all tokens of your love which you are able to withhold. If you find pleasure in not exerting yourself to write to me, I shall find pleasure in seeking out excuses for you. My desire to forgive all your faults is great.

A French officer was kind enough to talk about you to me for more than three hours this morning. He told me that France had concluded the peace. If this is true, could you not come to see me and take me back to your country with you? But no, I do not deserve that. Do whatever seems best to you; my love no longer depends upon the way in which you treat me.

Since you went away I have not had a moment of health, and nothing gives me any pleasure but to say your name over and over a thousand times a day. Some of the nuns, who know of the pitiable state to which you have reduced me, often come and talk to me of you.

I leave my room as little as possible – this room in which you have come to see me so many times. And I look continually at your portrait, which is dearer to me than life itself. It gives me some pleasure . . . but it also gives me pain when I think that I may never see you again. Why . . . how can it be that I shall never see you again? Have you abandoned me forever? I am in despair . . . your poor Mariana can write no more. A faintness is coming over her. . . . Farewell, farewell . . . take pity on me. . . .

Fifth letter (extract)

I write you for the last time . . . and I hope you will understand from the difference in expression and from the entire tone of this letter that you have finally convinced me you no longer love me, and that therefore I should no longer love you.

At the first opportunity I shall send you everything of yours that I still have. Do not fear that I shall write to you . . . I shall not even write your name upon the package. I have asked Dona Brites to take care of all that. She is accustomed to being my confidante, although of course in matters very different from this, and I can depend upon her more than upon myself. She will take all the necessary precautions to assure me that you have received the portrait and the bracelets you have given me.

For you must know that for several days I have felt myself capable of burning or destroying those tokens of your love which were so dear to me. But I have up to now shown so much weakness that you would not have believed that I could take such extreme measures. From the very pain it has cost me to part with them I wish nevertheless to extract a kind of pleasure, and I will at least cause you some vexation.

I confess, to our mutual shame, that I was more attached to these silly things than I should like to say; I felt that I had to go over all my thoughts again in order to free myself from each separately; and that at a time when I was congratulating myself on being finally free from you. But what cannot one accomplish when all the evidence points to the one hard conclusion? And so I have given everything over to Dona Brites. My God! the tears it cost me to bring myself to this. You can have no idea of the thousand uncertainties that can rage within one, and I shall certainly not recount them to you. . . .

Translated by Donald E. Erikson

WINNIE MANDELA (*b.* 1934)
South Africa

Winnie Mandela was born Nomzamo Winifred Madikizela in a small village in the Transkei. After studying at Johannesburg she became the first black woman social worker in South Africa. In 1958 she married Nelson Mandela, and during his political imprisonment from 1963 onwards she earned herself the reputation as 'the Mother of a Nation' for her part as Mandela's co-worker, continuing the fight against apartheid, despite continual harassment, detention and banishment to the Orange Free State by the South African government.

History has recently rewritten the story of Winnie Mandela, no longer a Mother but a monster, following disclosures about her 'football team' (a group of heavies who ran amok in her household, and were puportedly under her direct command). Winnie was implicated in the death of a fourteen-year-old township boy, Stompie Moeketsie, but the case remained unresolved. Shortly after the release from prison for which Nelson and Winnie had waited so long, they were divorced. Remarkably, in the last couple of years Winnie's career has made a dramatic recovery. Following the country's first democratic elections she was unexpectedly appointed as a Deputy Minister in the new government.

The following letter was written in 1985, after over twenty years of enforced separation.

To Nelson Mandela

20.2.85

I returned in the early hours of today after almost three sad weeks of the most emotional storms in our life of separation. I however had one thing to look forward to, the letter from you which I knew would make my year. I knew it would reconstruct my shattered soul and restore it to my faith – the nation. Moments of such self-indulgence bring shame to me at such times when I think of those who have paid the supreme price for their ideological beliefs. Some of those fallen ones were dearer to me than my own life.

The letter was there, dated 4.2.85. I'm rereading it for the umpteenth time. Contrary to your speculation at first, I do not think I would have had the fibre to bear it all if you had been with me. You once said I should expect the inevitable fact that the struggle leaves debris behind; from that moment those many years ago I swore to my infinitesimal ego that I would never allow myself to be part of that political quagmire.

If life is comprised of the things you enumerate and hold dear, I am lost for words due to the fact that in my own small way life feels a little more monumental, material and demanding of one's innermost soul. That is why the love and warmth that exude from you behind those unkind concrete grey monotonous and cruel walls simply overwhelms me, especially when I think of those who in the name of the struggle have been deprived of that love.

You refer to moments when love and happiness, trust and hope have turned into pure agony, when conscience and sense of guilt have ravaged every part of your being. It is true, darling, I've lost so much of what is dearest to me in the years of our separation. When you have lived alone as I've done as a young bride and never known what married life is all about you cling to minute consolations, the sparing of one from the indignities that ravage us. In our case, with all those we have lost, the dignity of death has been respected. . . .

I was so proud of your message to us. I've often wondered how I would have reacted if I had met you, Uncle Walter and others on the Pollsmoor steps and was told to take you home. . . .

LADY NIJŌ (13th Century)
Japan

Lady Nijōs autobiography, written in 1307, documenting the years 1271 to 1306 but discovered and translated only this century, has been acclaimed as one of the earliest and finest works of its kind. It tells the story of a young Japanese girl who becomes a concubine at the age of fourteen. Lady Nijō details her many illicit love affairs with emperors, statesmen and priests, her eventual expulsion from court and her subsequent travels as a Buddhist nun. In her account she includes letters that were sent to her, and her replies, written in the traditional Japanese style of a poem.

At the time of writing, in 1272, Lady Nijō's father has just died and the court is in mourning. Sometimes Lady Nijō gives the name of the lover she is writing to, but here she is mysterious, writing to 'someone who had inquired about me every day since my father had died', and who 'came to visit me by moonlight'.

1272

To that other parting
Is added today's farewell:
On sleeves already damp
Still more dew falls.

Autumn dew falls on every tree
On every blade of grass:
How could anyone claim
It's only on our sleeves?

To Kameyama 1275

Reality or a dream
What does it matter?
Cherry blossoms bloom but to fall
In this fleeting world.

To Emperor GoFukakusa 1281

How much longer will pity
Lead you to this garden,
As choked with weeds
As my thoughts with pain?

To Iinuma 1289

Our parting now will dampen
Rumors we have not denied.
This gown will rot away
From tears of intense longing.

Translated by Karen Brazell

ANON., MINER'S WIFE, 1914
England

This moving letter from a bereaved wife to her husband was written after his death in a mining disaster at Whitehaven in 1914.

To a husband

. . . God took my man but I could never forget him he was the best man that ever lived at least I thought that, maybe it was just that I got the right kind of man. We had been married for 25 years and they were hard years at that, many a thing we both done without for the sake of the children. We had 11 and if I had him back I would live the same life over again. Just when we were beginning to stand on our feet I lost him I can't get over it when I think of him how happy he was that morning going to work and telling me he would hurry home, but I have been waiting a long time now. At night when I am sitting and I hear clogs coming down the street I just sit and wait hoping they are coming to my door, then they go right on and my heart is broke.

LADY EMMA HAMILTON (1763–1815)
France

Emma Hart, later Lady Hamilton, was a one-time servant maid who became a society beauty, attracting the adulation of the painter George Romney, and stimulating a flurry of portraits of her. Her other conquests included Sir William Hamilton, Admiral Nelson and Charles Greville MP, whom she is addressing here. She died in poverty and neglect at Calais in 1815. (See also her letter to Nelson in ***Celebration****.)*

To Hon. Charles Greville, MP

The Bacchante
Naples, July 22, 1786

My ever dearest Greville, – I am now onely writing to beg of you for God's sake to send me one letter, if it is onely a farewell. Sure I have deserved this, for the sake of the love you once had for me. . . . So, pray, let me beg of you, my much loved Greville, only one line from your dear, dear hands. You don't know how thankful I shall be for it. For if you knew the misery [I] feel, oh! your heart would not be intirely shut up against me; for I love you with the truest affection. Don't let anybody sett you against me. Some of your friends – your foes, perhaps; I don't know what to stile them – have long wisht me ill. But, Greville, you never will meet with anybody that has a truer affection for you than I have, and I onely wish it was in my power to shew you what I could do for you. As soon as I know your determination I shall take my own measures. If I don't hear from you, and that you are coming according to promise, I shall be in England at Christmas at farthest. Don't be unhappy at that. I will see you once more, for the last time, I find life is unsupportable without you. Oh, my heart is intirely broke. Then, for God's sake, my ever dear Greville, do write to me some comfort. I don't know what to do. I am now in that state I am incapable of anything. I have [a] language-master, a singing-master, musick, etc., but what is it for? If it was to amuse you, I should be happy. But, Greville, what will it avail me? I am poor, helpeless and forlorn. . . . But no more, I will trust to providence; and wherever you go, God bless you and preserve you, and may you allways be happy!

SIMONE DE BEAUVOIR (1908–86)
France

*De Beauvoir's use of the word 'little' – as in 'little arm', 'little one', 'little Poulpiquet' – occurs so frequently in her letters to Sartre that it has been the subject of a French thesis, hinting at various interpretations. (See also **Temptation** and **Frustration**.)*

To Jean-Paul Sartre

Hôtel de Bretagne, Douarnenez
Monday 25 September [1939]

My love, my dear love
My heart's just a mush this evening, I'm consumed by passion for you and it couldn't be more painful. This has been brewing all day and it came down on me like a tornado in the streets of Douarnenez, where I broke into sobs. Luckily it was moonlight! My love, we were together on this little bridge where there were lots of fishermen in red trousers sitting in a row on the parapet. And just now I missed your little arm in mine and your face beside me so strongly that I didn't know what was to become of me. I've revisited Locronan – I remember it all so well. How, on the beach of St Anne de la Palud, you told me about Isoré and his loves. How, on the bay at Douarnenez, near a pine wood that I've seen again, you told me that you loved to see the sea through the pine trees, and we talked about evolutionism and mechanicism and about animals. Every morning we'd wake up in our twin beds and I'd ask you: 'How are you, my little Poulpiquet?'. O my love, I do so long for your tenderness this evening! I feel I've never told you enough how I loved you, that I've never been nice enough to you. My sweet little one, how I'd like to hold you and cover you with kisses – how happy I've been with you! From all sides today the most heart-rending memories came crowding back to me.

I left this morning at 9 on a big red coach. We drove without stopping to Morgat, which I reached at 11. The route was very pretty – I really like all those Breton churches and villages – and Morgat's on a wonderful stretch of coast. I went off for a long walk all round the peninsula, which is densely covered with heather and broom. There are big sheer cliffs over a blue-and-green sea – marvellous. The sun was dazzling and I felt really intensely that particular nature of Brittany: a white background of sky, stone and water, and the presence of the sea everywhere among the moors, giving them their meaning. The people at the end of the peninsula are at least as wild as the old women of Emborio. Everywhere I was regarded as a spy, and people muttered in Breton as I passed. I walked, I was gripped by what I saw, and this mingled with the regret I was feeling for you – it was poetic and intense. From the tip of the peninsula, you were right opposite Camaret and could see the Tas-de-Pois where we went when it rained so hard. And what with the wind, and the sun on the sea, and the height of the cliffs, it was really exhilarating. And surrounded by all that I felt my heart softening. I took the coach again at 5. You had to change at Locronan, so I went for a meal of eggs and milk at our hotel. But it's no longer on the same premises, it's across the way, in a Renaissance house with a dining-room done up with greater pomp – and, it must be said, very successfully. But the old premises are still there, and I revisited the old dining-room where on one wet day we were all alone. Then I caught another coach, which brought me here. I took a room, then went down to the harbour. It was sunset, and at the same time there was moonlight: you'd have said a nocturnal landscape lit by some extraordinary artifice – I've never seen light like that. And how charming the little boats were, with their blue nets outspread! There were girls too on the jetty, laughing aloud, and nice young people strolling in groups who were laughing too. I hadn't heard anyone laugh in public, or sing, since the war started. It was one of the tenderest evenings of peace and happiness you could dream of. I strolled beside the sea till darkness fell completely, and cried like a baby. I love you, my beloved.

I came back here to write and am in the hotel café, where there's a collection of strange individuals. There's a bearded fellow with a contorted face who produces inarticulate sounds, and another bearded fellow in a pink shirt – they're playing piquet. It's only 8.30, but I'm going upstairs to read in bed. Tomorrow I'll go to the Pointe du Raz.

I received a charming letter from Kos. – but nothing from you either yesterday or today. I'd so like to find a way of seeing you. My beloved, I love you and I'd be so nice if you were there. You're my life, my happiness and my self. You're everything for me – and this evening, above all, a tender face that I can't think of without tears (in spite of the bearded fellows). I love you passionately.

Your charming Beaver

Write to me at 116 Rue d'Assas, c/o Mme Pardo.

Translated by Quintin Hoare

SOPHIA DOROTHEA OF ZELL, ELECTRESS OF HANOVER (1666–1727)
Germany

Married at age sixteen to Prince George Louis, who later became King George I of England. The loveless match produced two children: Sophia, who became mother of Frederick the Great, and George, who became King George II of England.

Two years after the birth of her second child, Sophia Dorothea – still only twenty-two, lively, lonely and frustrated – met the Swedish nobleman Count Philip Christopher von Koenigsmarck, who had been a childhood acquaintance. She soon began a difficult and dangerous love intrigue with the Count, which continued for two years, until Koenigsmarck was murdered on leaving her bedroom. Prince George (who had been openly unfaithful throughout their marriage) immediately divorced Sophia Dorothea amidst much scandal, and she was banished from public life.

The lovers sent their letters for safekeeping to Koenigsmarck's sister. After his murder a large number were seized and destroyed, but the following are amongst those remaining. They were translated by W.H. Wilkins in 1898.

To Philip von Koenigsmarck

Aht, July 1

I am *in extremis*, and the only thing that can save me is a few lines from your incomparable hand. If I had the good fortune to behold them I should forthwith be healed. I hope you will not be so cruel as to refuse me this favour, for, since it is you who cause my sufferings, it is only just that you should send me comfort. Were I not writing to one for whom my respect is as great as my love, I would find better terms to express my devotion; but, fearing to offend, I end here, only beseeching you not to forget me wholly, and to believe me always your slave.

Hanover, undated

I spent the stillness of the night without sleeping, and all the day thinking of you, weeping over our separation. Never did a day seem so long to me; I do not know how I shall ever get reconciled to your absence. La Gouvernante has just given me your letter; I received it with rapture. Rest assured I will do even more than I have promised, and lose no opportunity of showing you my love. If I could shut myself up while you are away and see no one, I would do so gladly, for without you everything is distasteful and wearisome. Nothing can make your absence bearable to me; I am faint with weeping. I hope to prove by my life that no woman has ever loved man as I love you, and no faithfulness will ever equal mine. In spite of every trial and all that may befall, nothing will sever me from you. Of a truth, dear one, my love will only end with my life.

I was so changed and depressed today that even the Prince, my husband, pitied me, and said I was ill and ought to take care of myself. He is right, – I am ill; but my illness comes only from loving you, and I never wish to be cured. I have not seen anyone worth mentioning. I went to visit the Duchess (Sophia) for a little while but returned home as soon as possible to have the joy of talking about you. La Gazelle's husband came to wish me goodbye; I saw him in my chamber, and he kissed my hand.

It is now eight o'clock, and I must go and pay my court. How dull I shall seem! – how stupid! I shall withdraw immediately after supper, so that I may have the pleasure of reading your letters again, the only pleasure I have while you are away. Farewell, my worshipped one. Only death will sever me from you; all human powers will never succeed. Remember all your promises, and be as constant as I will be faithful.

(Extract)

Zell
July 25
August 4

This is the third post, and still no letter! Surely so tender a lover as you always seemed to be cannot have wholly forgotten me – or are we betrayed? It positively must be one thing or the other. The suspense is so acute that I have not a moment's peace. But my great fear is that you have changed. I think of nothing else, nor of all that may happen to me. Is it possible that you have forgotten your vows of eternal fidelity? I strive to drive away my sad thoughts, but I am in such abject melancholy that I fear it is a foreboding of misfortune. If you love me no longer I shall never be comforted. But what is the use of telling you that?

Hanover, August 5

This is the sixth day since you left, and I have not had a word from you. What neglect and what disdain! In what way have I deserved such treatment? Is it for loving you to adoration, for having sacrificed everything? But of what use to remind you of this? My suspense is worse than death; nothing can equal the torments this cruel anxiety makes me suffer. What an ill fate is mine, good God! What shame to love without being loved! I was born to love you, and I shall love you as long as I live. If it be true that you have changed, and I have no end of reasons for fearing so, I wish you no punishment save that of never finding, wherever you may be, a love and fidelity equal to mine. I wish, despite the pleasures of fresh conquests, you may never cease to regret the love and tenderness that I have shown you. You will never find in the whole world anyone so loving and so sincere. I love you more than woman has ever loved man. But I tell you the same things too often; you must be tired of them. Do not count it ill, I implore you, nor grudge me the sad consolation of complaining of your harshness. I am very anxious for fear they have detained the letter you were to have written to me from Zell. I have not received a word; everything conspires to crush me. Perhaps in addition to the fact that you no longer love me, I am on the eve of being utterly lost. It is too much all at once; I shall break down under it. I must end this tomorrow; I shall go to Communion. Farewell. I forgive you all you make me suffer.

Translated by W.H. Wilkins

KWEI-LI (19th Century)
China

(See also **Declaration**.)

To her husband, written on the death of her child

My son, my man-child is dead. The life has gone from his body, the breath from his lips. I have held him all the night close to my heart and it does not give him warmth. They have taken him from me and told me he has gone to the Gods. There are no Gods. There are no Gods. I am alone.

[. . .]

He had thine eyes – he was like to thee. Thou wilt never know thy son and mine, my Springtime. Why could they not have left thy son for thee to see? He was so strong and beautiful, my first-born.

[. . .]

Do not chide me. I cannot write. What do I do? I do not know. I lie long hours and watch the tiny mites that live within the sun's bright golden rays, and say, 'Why could I not exchange my womanhood, that hopes and loves and sorrows, for one of those small dancing spots within the sunbeams? At least they do not feel.'

Translated by Elizabeth Cooper

CELEBRATION:
'All last night I was with you in happy dreams'

VALENTINE ACKLAND (1906–68)
England

Valentine Ackland was born in London to a wealthy family, and drifted through a bohemian London of the 1920s until she met and fell in love with writer Sylvia Townsend Warner, in 1930. Their celebrated liaison endured until Ackland's death in 1968. The following letter forms the preface to Ackland's autobiography: For Sylvia: An Honest Account.

To Sylvia Townsend Warner

Frome Vauchurch 4 July 1949

My Love,
I have finished this tonight, as best I can; and it is for you. It is strange to think that probably this is all I have given you, this record of blundering from shame to shame, with so much glory shining down on me all the time, and most brightly from you, who are my sun.

I forgot to put in the secular quotation which stands best for us, and has been sword and shield to me ever since you wrote it down in pencil on the flyleaf of the book you gave me for Christmas, 1930: 'Never heed,' said the girl, 'I'll stand by you.' I'm a coward, my Love, and I have heeded far too often, but that has made no difference to the truth of this that you wrote down for me: let it be true to our lives' end, Sylvia –

Valentine – who loves you.

LADY EMMA HAMILTON (1763–1815)
France

(See also **Desolation**)

This letter was returned unopened on account of Nelson's death.

To Lord Nelson

Canterbury, October 8, 1805

Dearest husband of my heart, – You are all in this world to your Emma – may God send you victory and Honour [and] soon to your *Emma, Horatia and paradise Merton*, for when you are there it will be paradise. *My* own Nelson. May God prosper you and preserve you for the sake of your affectionate

Emma

EMPRESS JOSÉPHINE (1763–1814)
France

Joséphine de Beauharnais met Napoleon Bonaparte when he was a young general of twenty-six, she a 'society lady' of thirty-two. Fifteen days after their first meeting (in 1795) they became lovers, and six months later they were married. They were frequently separated, and during these times Napoleon inundated the Empress with letters.

The marriage was rocky with infidelities on both sides. They were divorced in 1810, when the following poignant letter was sent from Joséphine to Napoleon.

To Napoleon Bonaparte

Navarra, April 1810

A thousand, thousand tender thanks for not having forgotten me. My son has just brought me your letter. With what ardour I read it and yet I spent much time on it; for there was not a word in it that did not make me weep. But those tears were so sweet. I found again my whole heart, and such as it will always be; there are sentiments which are life itself, and which can only finish with it.

I would be in despair if my letter of the 19th had displeased you; I do not entirely remember its expressions, but I know what very painful sentiment had dictated it, it was the chagrin not to have had news from you.

I had written you at my departure from Malmaison; and since then, how many times did I not wish to write to you! But I felt the reason of your silence, and I feared to be importunate by a letter. Yours has been a balm for me. Be happy; be it as much as you deserve it; it is my entire heart that speaks to you. You also have just given me my share of happiness, and a share very vividly felt; nothing can equal the value for me of a mark of your remembrance.

Adieu, my friend; I thank you as tenderly as I shall always love you.

Joséphine

VITA SACKVILLE-WEST (1892–1962)
England

(See also **Invitation**, **Declaration**, **Consummation** and **Desolation**.)

To Violet Trefusis

September 3, 1950

My darling,
It was a real event in my life and my heart to be with you the other day. We do matter to each other, don't we? however much our ways may have diverged. I think we have got something indestructible between us, haven't we? Even right back to the library seat in your papa's room at Grosvenor Street – and then at Duntreath – and then to everything that came afterwards. *Glissons, mortels* . . . but what a bond, Lushka darling; a bond of childhood and subsequent passion, such as neither of us will ever share with anyone else.

It has been a very strange relationship, ours; unhappy at times, happy at others; but unique in its way, and infinitely precious to me and (may I say?) to you.

What I like about it is that we always come together again however long the gaps in our meetings may have been. Time seems to make no difference. This is a sort of love letter I suppose. Odd that I should be writing you a love letter after all these years – when we have written so many to each other. *Parceque c'était lui, parceque c'était moi.**

Oh, you sent me a book about Elizabeth Barrett Browning. Thank you, darling generous Lushka and you gave me a coal-black briquet. It lights up into the flame of love which always burns in my heart whenever I think of you. You said it would last for three months, but our love has lasted for forty years and more.

Your
Mitya

*Because it was him, because it was me.

MARY WOLLSTONECRAFT (1759–97)
England

(See also **Consummation**.)

To Gilbert Imlay

Paris, 1793, Friday Morning

I am glad to find that other people can be unreasonable as well as myself; for be it known to thee that I answered thy *first* letter the very night it reached me (Sunday), though thou couldst not receive it before Wednesday, because it was not sent off till the next day. There is a full, true, and particular account.

Yet I am not angry with thee, my love, for I think that it is a proof of stupidity, and likewise of a milk-and-water affection, which comes to the same thing when the temper is governed by a square and compass. There is nothing picturesque in this straight-lined equality, and the passions always give grace to the actions.

Recollection now makes my heart bound to thee; but it is not to thy money-getting face, though I cannot be seriously displeased with the exertion which increases my esteem, or rather is what I should have expected from thy character. No; I have thy honest countenance before me – relaxed by tenderness; a little – little wounded by my whims; and thy eyes glittering with sympathy. Thy lips then feel softer than soft, and I rest my cheek on thine, forgetting all the world. I have not left the hue of love out of the picture – the rosy glow; and fancy has spread it over my own cheeks, I believe, for I feel them burning, whilst a delicious tear trembles in my eye that would be all your own, if a grateful emotion directed to the Father of nature, who has made me thus alive to happiness, did not give more warmth to the sentiment it divides. I must pause a moment.

Need I tell you that I am tranquil after writing thus? I do not know why, but I have more confidence in your affection, when absent, than present; nay, I think that you must love me, for, in the sincerity of my heart let me say it, I believe I deserve your tenderness, because I am true, and have a degree of sensibility that you can see and relish.

Yours sincerely,

Mary

MAUD GONNE (1867–1953)
England

(See also **Consummation**.)

To W.B. Yeats

13 Rue de Passy
Paris
Friday [December 1908]

Dearest

It was hard leaving you yesterday, but I knew it would be just as hard today if I had waited. Life is so good when we are together & we are together so little –!

Did you know it I went to you last night? about 12 or 2 o'clock I don't exactly know the time. I think you knew. It was as it was when you made me see with the golden light on Wednesday. I shall go to you again often but not quite in that way, I shall try to make strong & well for your work for dear one you must work or I shall begin tormenting myself thinking perhaps I help to make you idle & then I would soon feel we ought not to meet at all, & that would be O so dreary! –

You asked me yesterday if I am not a little sad that things are as they are between us – I am sorry & I am glad. It is hard being away from each other so much there are moments when I am dreadfully lonely & long to be with you, – one of these moments is on me now – but beloved I am glad & proud beyond measure of your love, & that it is strong enough & high enough to accept the spiritual love & union I offer –

I have prayed so hard to have all earthly desire taken from my love for you & dearest, loving you as I do, I have prayed & I am praying still that the bodily desire for me may be taken from you too. I know how hard & rare a thing it is for a man to hold spiritual love when the bodily desire is gone & I have not made these prayers without a terrible struggle a struggle that shook my life though I do not speak much of it & generally manage to laugh.

That struggle is over & I have found peace. I think today I could let you marry another without losing it – for I know the spiritual union between us will outlive this life, even if we never see each other in this world again.

Write to me soon.

Yours

Maud

Thursday
On the boat going to Ireland
[May 1909]

Beloved
I write to you things I wanted to say & could not. All last night I was with you in happy dreams, not that great spiritual union of which I once wrote, but I know we were together & at peace & I hope that peace came to you too. Dearest I have not come to the decision I have come to without struggle & without suffering though once that decision come to, in answer to my prayers, the suffering & the struggle ceased in a way I surely do not deserve. Beloved I will pray with my whole strength that suffering & temptation may be taken from you as they have from me & that we may gain spiritual union stronger than earthly union could ever be.

I want to thank you my own for being generous with me *as you have always been.* I have brought suffering to you so often, & you never reproach me. – Will I ever bring you happiness & peace to compensate? I pray to God that by holding our love pure it may be so.

Some of the things I said to you yesterday evening were unjust, *I had no right* to say them, and I am sorry I did – On me alone the blame lies for the forgetfulness of that spiritual marriage long ago, which if we had obeyed would have saved us both from the long weariness of separation.

I was carried away on the wave of hate which I thought righteous, I sought a wild revenge which because impersonal I thought noble. I forgot that those who would distribute life or death must be purer than the angels & that I was full of human passion & weakness.

Willie your arms were not strong enough to save me for my eyes were too blind to see these things & all the crushing sorrow that came on me *I have earned.*

My loved one I belong to you more in this renunciation than if I came to you in sin. Did you not say yourself that our love must be holy?

Yours

Maud

ANON., POLITICAL PRISONER (TWENTIETH CENTURY) USSR

When you read this letter I shall already be home!!!

Greetings from here for the final time, my darling!

This is the last letter from your captive love! . . . God, tomorrow! Tomorrow morning I shall be walking away from here, leaving this Hell. First I shall walk, and then I shall fly. I shall be met, the air ticket is already booked and then – up, up and away – to home – and then: to you.

I don't know what to write. The last few days have been an awful turmoil. The local officials have caused me a pile of problems, of course, which I can't bring myself to write about now – I'll tell you all about it later. But the fact that tomorrow I shall walk out of the compound gates along with the other women is all thanks to my faithful friends. In short, nearly every day there have been attempts to put me into SHIZO and even straight into PKT (and that would be very dangerous). But. . . . What would I have done if over these last two years practically half the compound hadn't become my friends? So the authorities held back, cried off – obviously an order had arrived from above telling them not to make a big fuss. But they've certainly taken their toll on my nerves.

Oh to the dogs with them all! Or maybe not! I'd feel sorry for the dogs. They'd eat them whole, tails and all. Taking everything into consideration, to Hell with them! I would express myself more strongly, but, in the first place, you don't approve of women swearing, and in the second place it's a pity somehow to use the language of the camp less than twenty-four hours before being freed. Let's leave them to their own fate.

Are there really only a couple of days to go before . . . ?

No, darling. I won't go to your relatives on the first day. There's mother: I shall spend the first day with my own family. And then the day after (God, it's only the day after tomorrow – God willing, of course!) I shall visit your family first thing in the morning. I hope that there will already be a letter there waiting for me. I will visit your home, go into your room, see first of all 'Night', 'Self-Portrait', 'Woman Who Has Lost Her Child', 'Vision', and then find the letter for me on your desk . . . I shall sit, in convict fashion, on the floor, open the envelope and begin to read the letter, and Cheshka the dog will come over to me, lick my ear and lie down beside me. And I shall read out to her what her master says. I wonder whether Cheshka will recognise me? Or whether she will suddenly detect an unfamiliar scent and bark at me.

No, I am simply not in a condition to write. Forgive me, my darling. And everyone is pestering me to say goodbye to them, and I've still got a hundred and one things to do, like passing on my final 'collections' for prior transmission to freedom – letters, a few poems, etc. and then I need to give away all my possessions so as not to upset anyone, and then memorise all the commissions and requests – there's no way I could take a list out with me. And then, of course, there's the farewell supper – the usual custom!

Translated by Julia Voznesenskaya

ANNE LOUISE GERMAINE DE STAËL (1766–1817)
France

Daughter of Jacques Necker, the great French financier under Louis XVI, she had to flee at the outbreak of the French Revolution. Her marriage to de Staël was unhappy, so she cultivated her life in a Parisian salon, where she met many admirers. In 1794 she took up with Benjamin Constant (a man badly misnamed), to whom she is writing here.

To Benjamin Constant

October 1st, 1804

Dear Friend, – Rejoice with me if Providence allows me to descend before you into the tomb. After the death of my father, I could not possibly endure yours. I shall follow the admirable man, beloved of you, and shall await you there with a heart, which God will pardon, because it has loved much. Look after my children! In the letter which you are to show them, I exhort them to love in you, a man whom their mother has loved so much. Ah! this word 'loved' that was our fate, what does it mean in the hereafter? My father's Creator is a kind Being. Pray to Him, my friend, through Him the dead stands in communication with the living. You know that by an arrangement between us a house bought by M. Fourcault for Madame de Nassau in the Rue des Mathuzins belongs to us, both under the stipulations that the interest belongs to you, and the capital, after you, to my daughter. If you would rather sell it, you must invest the money in a way approved of by the guardians, but the interest remains yours to your death. Farewell, my dear Benjamin, I hope that you at least will be near me when I die. Oh, I did not close my father's eyes: will you close mine?

Necker Staël de Holstein

ANNE SEXTON (1928–74)
USA

Those close to Anne Sexton had always known she would commit suicide. She was thorough in her preparations for her death, asking particular friends which of her possessions they would like, selecting a biographer and preparing her manuscripts for the Boston University archive. As early as April 1969 she wrote the following letter to her daughter, a moving anticipation of her daughter's grief and an attempt to hold and comfort her. (See also ***Adulation****.)*

To Linda Gray Sexton

Wed – 2:45 p.m.

Dear Linda,
I am in the middle of a flight to St. Louis to give a reading. I was reading a *New Yorker* story that made me think of my mother and all alone in the seat I whispered to her 'I know Mother, I know.' (Found a pen!) And I thought of you – someday flying somewhere all alone and me dead perhaps and you wishing to speak to me.

And I want to speak back. (Linda, maybe it won't be flying, maybe it will be at your *own* kitchen table drinking tea some afternoon when you are 40. *Anytime.*) – I want to say back.

1st I love you.
2. You *never* let me down.
3. I know. I was there once. I *too*, was 40 and with a dead mother who I needed still. [. . .]

This is my message to the 40-year-old Linda. No matter what happens you were always my bobolink, my special Linda Gray. Life is not easy. It is awfully lonely. *I* know that. Now you too know it – wherever you are, Linda, talking to me. But I've had a good life – I wrote unhappy – but I lived to the hilt. You too, Linda – Live to the HILT! To the top. I love you, 40-year-old Linda, and I love what you do, what you find, what you are! – Be your own woman. Belong to those you love. Talk to my poems, and talk to your heart – I'm in both: if you need me. I lied, Linda. I did love my mother and she loved me. She never held me but I miss her, so that I have to deny I ever loved her – or she me! Silly Anne! So there!

xoxoxo
Mom

ELEANOR MABEL SARTON (1878–?)
USA

Eleanor Mabel Sarton arrived in the USA from Belgium as a refugee in 1916. These exquisitely tender love letters to her daughter, the renowned Canadian writer May Sarton, were published by May Sarton in 1986. The first is written to May as a little girl of five around the year 1922; the second to the grown-up May, then aged twenty-eight.

To May Sarton

[Undated]

Dear little daughter,
I have written a long letter to Daddy and not a word in it for you – but now here is a little letter all for yourself. Daddy says you are *so* good that he has to tell you so sometimes – Mother is so glad! She often and often says to herself – is Baby May sleeping? – is she happy and good? – does she ask to be put in her chair when it's necessary? – does she eat up her food nicely? – and a hundred other questions. When Mother thinks of you, it is as if a smile came to her from somewhere mysterious each time. Little May, little May, you are so dear to us already – shall we someday be very dear to *you*? – be your best friends? – you must help us you know. We will try to love you for yourself and not for us – try to be really 'near' you and not misunderstand when you will think differently to us because you will be young and we shall be old.

But I am thinking a long way ahead – and just now I would be quite content to feel your little arms tight round my neck and see you smile at me. You won't have forgotten me will you when I come back, little girlie?

Now goodbye, daughter of ours – go on being very quiet and good so Daddy can write and Mother not fret about you both. Fais '*lievekes*'* à Daddy pour mois puis que je ne suis pas là pour l'embrasser.

Mother

*Flemish for a light kiss.

Friday Even.
[6 July 1945]

O my darling, my poet-child, I am thinking of you with particular tenderness because I heard an hour ago from R.W.B. that Harpers* had turned down the book. Yes – it is a blow – (to me too) – but suddenly on its heels comes such a surge of pride & *sureness* of you that I must interrupt the 'supper getting' & leave the salad to itself for just a moment to pour out a little of the over-flow. There has been a violent thunder storm with tremendous wind pulling at the trees & heavy rain beating at everything – but now the air is calm & still & the sky is filled with tiny silvery white clouds, and the trees stand in grandeur & peace. My heart & my mind somehow are filled with this – and I wish I could enfold it in words that would bring some of it to you – the peace and patience that complete faith in someone always follow upon a storm of disappointment or any blow dealt them.

I do love you so *proudly*,

Mother

***The Bridge of Years* later published by Doubleday, 1946

COLETTE (1873–1954)
France

(See also **Declaration**.)

To Marguerite Moreno

Kensington Hôtel, La Croix (Var), January 3, 1928

. . . Moonlight, a wood fire, my own good lamp. What can I complain about? Only the absence of those I love.

My daughter writes me charming loving letters. The last contained this: 'Papa isn't looking well. He has too much blood sugar! Your prediction was right!' Sugar isn't good for Jouvenel. He's a man who scourges himself. But I must repeat something his own mother – the one we call Mamita – said to my daughter in private a month or so ago. Mamita had been ill herself. 'I'm getting better,' she said. 'But your father – oh yes, your father – he's much sicker than I. I've had his blood analyzed . . .' And she stopped, with an air of mystery and delectation. What a smoldering old log! What a destructive flame!

For the new year, my Marguerite, I wish you – whatever suits you best. The same torments – less sharp, less attached to the state of health of your 'bad boy' Pierre; the same joys indissolubly mixed with the same torments – all to continue as they have been. Isn't that better than any change? I also wish you wealth and tranquillity – and at the same time your work. Yes, of course, I'm being contradictory. But I am not illogical. And I love you tenderly. Oh, how happy I'd be to have you here for a few days!

To Jean Cocteau (on the death of Marguerite Moreno)

Grasse, late July 1948

Dear Jean, how right you were to write me. To you I can say the truth – that I don't know how I shall get used to her dying. Fifty-four years of friendship! And not an easy or unbroken friendship, by any means! A friendship which was threatened, which might have perished, but which survived everything. . . .

Translated by Robert Phelps

EMILY DICKINSON (1830–86)
USA

(See also **Invitation**, **Adulation** and **Consummation**.)

To Susan Gilbert (Dickinson)

1886

To Sue
You must let me go first, Sue, because I live in the sea always and know the road. I would have drowned twice to save you sinking, dear, if I could only have covered your eyes so you wouldn't have seen the water.
Sue,
The tie between us is very fine, but a hair never dissolves.
Lovingly,

Emily

ACKNOWLEDGEMENTS

Every effort has been made to trace copyright holders in all copyright material in this book. In the event of any oversight the editor would like to apologise sincerely, and suggest that the publisher be contacted. The following sources and permissions are gratefully acknowledged:

Letters of Anon., miner's wife and Violet Coward from *A Letter Doesn't Blush,* edited by Nicholas Parsons, Buchan & Enright, London.

Letters of Elizabeth Barrett Browning from *Letters of Robert and Elizabeth Barrett Browning*, published by John Murray Ltd.

Letters of Simone de Beauvoir from *Letters to Sartre*, translated and edited by Quintin Hoare, with an introduction by Sylvie Le Bon de Beauvoir. First published in Great Britain by Radius, 1991. Reprinted by permission Hutchinson Ltd.

Letter of Mary Bicknell to John Constable from *Memoirs of the Life of John Constable* by C.R. Leslie, BPC publishers, John Lehmann, 1949.

Letters of Anne Boleyn and Queen Elizabeth I from The Harleian 4031, folio 4 and Harleian 36, folio 268. Reprinted by permission The Trustees of the British Museum.

Letters of Charlotte Brontë from *The Letters of Charlotte Brontë 1816–1855*, edited by Clement Shorter.

Letters of Jane Welsh Carlyle from *Jane Welsh Carlyle: A New Selection of her Letters*, edited by Trudy Bliss, published by Victor Gollancz Ltd, 1953.

Letters of Colette from *Letters from Colette* (Virago Press), selected and translated by Robert Phelps, reprinted by permission Farrar, Straus & Giroux Inc.

Letters of Emily Dickinson from *The Letters of Emily Dickinson*, edited by Maria Dickinson Bianchi, 1932.

Letters of Sophia Dorothea of Zell from *The Love of an Uncrowned Queen 1900*. Translated by W.H. Wilkins, published by Hutchinson Ltd.

Letters of Ninon de L'Enclos from *Correspondance authentique de Ninon de L'Enclos* 1886, Émile Colombey, Paris.

Letters of Anne Kramer (*née* Gudis) from *Since You Went Away*, edited by J.B. Litoff and David C. Smith and published by Oxford University Press. Copyright © Anne Kramer.

Letters of Marietta Machiavelli and Ippolita Torelli, published in the Italian in *The Gentlest Art: Letters in Renaissance Italy*, edited by K.T. Butler, translated by Jamie McKendrick. Copyright © this translation, Jamie McKendrick 1994.

Letters of Lady Emma Hamilton from *The Life and Letters of Lady Hamilton*, edited by Hugh Tours, 1963, and published by Victor Gollancz Ltd.

Letters from Maud Gonne from *The Gonne–Yeats Letters 1893–1938* (Pimlico), edited with an introduction by Anna MacBride White and A. Norman Jeffries. Copyright © Anna MacBride White 1992. Reprinted by permission Hutchinson Ltd.

Letter of Lady Mary Elcho from *The Letters of Arthur Balfour and Lady Elcho 1885–1917*, edited by Jane Ridley and Clayre Percy (Hamish Hamilton 1992.) Copyright © Jane Ridley and Clayre Percy, 1992. Reprinted by permission.

'Letter to Haruko' by June Jordan, from *Haruko/Love Poetry* by June Jordan, published by Virago Press. Copyright © June Jordan 1992, reprinted by permission the author and Virago Press.

Letters of Kwei-li from *The Love Letters of a Chinese Lady*, translated by Elizabeth Cooper. Published by TN Foulis, 1919.

Letter of Winnie Mandela from *Part of My Soul* by Winnie Mandela, edited by Anne Benjamin, adapted by Mary Benson (Penguin Books 1985) copyright © Rowohlt Taschenbuch Verlag GmbH 1984, reprinted by permission Penguin Books Ltd.

Letters of Katherine Mansfield from *Letters of Katherine Mansfield to John Middleton Murry*, edited by J.M. Murry, (1928, 1929). Reprinted by permission The Society of Authors as the literary representatives of the Estate of Katherine Mansfield.

Letters of Mary Meigs copyright © 1992 Mary Meigs, reprinted by kind permission of the author.

Letters of Mileva Marić from *The Letters of Albert Einstein and Mileva Marić*, edited by Jürgen Rein and Robert Schulmann, translated from the German by Shawn Smith and published by Princeton University Press in 1992. Reprinted by permission Princeton University Press.

Letter of Lady Mary Wortley Montagu from *The Complete Letters of Lady Mary Wortley Montagu*, edited by Robert Halsband, vol. 1 (1965). Reprinted by permission the publisher, Oxford University Press.

Letters of Suniti Namjoshi and Gillian Hanscombe from *Flesh and Paper* by Namjoshi and Hanscombe, Jezebel Press, Seaton, Devon, 1986. Reprinted by kind permission and copyright © Namjoshi and Hanscombe.

Letter of a Portuguese Nun, Mariana Alcoforado, from *Lettres portugaises* (1669), translated in 1893 by Edgar Prestage.

Letter of political prisoner in the USSR from *Letters of Love*, edited by Julia Voznesenskaya, first published in English by Quartet Books Ltd, 1989. Reprinted by permission Quartet Books Ltd.

Letters of Lady Nijō from *The Confessions of Lady Nijō*, translated by Karen Brazell. Copyright © Karen Brazell 1973, reprinted by permission Peter Owen Publishers, London.

Letters of Anaïs Nin from *A Literate Passion*, edited and with an introduction by Gunther Stuhlmann, Allison & Busby 1988. Copyright © the letters, Rupert Pole as Trustee of the last will and testament of Anaïs Nin.

Letters of Vita Sackville-West reprinted by kind permission the Executor, Nigel Nicolson.

Letters of George Sand from *Correspondances de George Sand et de Alfred de Musset*, edited by Félix Decori, Brussels, 1904.

Letters of Eleanor Sarton from *Letters to May by Eleanor May Sarton*

(1878–1950), Puckerbrush Press, Orono, Maine, 1986. Reprinted by kind permission, and copyright © 1992, her daughter, May Sarton.

Letters of Anne Sexton from *Anne Sexton: A Self-Portrait in Letters*, edited and introduced by Linda Sexton and Lois Ames, copyright © 1977 by Linda Gray Sexton and Loring Conant Jr., executors of the will of Anne Sexton. Reprinted by permission of Sterling Lord Literistic, Inc. All rights reserved.

Letter of Minna Simmons from *Dear Girl: The Diaries and Letters of Two Working Women 1897–1917*, edited by Tierl Thompson, copyright © Tierl Thompson 1987. Reprinted by permission The Women's Press Ltd, 34 Great Sutton Street, London EC1V ODX.

Letter of Maria del Socorro, 21 December 1988 © 1992 Larry Siems, from *Between the Lines*, edited by Larry Siems, published by The Ecco Press. Reprinted by permission.

Letter of Nkweto wa Chilinda copyright © Nkweto wa Chilinda 1992, reprinted by kind permission the author.

Letters of Freya Stark from O*ver the Rim of the World*, by Freya Stark, ed. Caroline Moorhead. Reprinted by permission John Murray (Publishers) Ltd.

Letters of Edith Thompson from *The Trial of Frederick Bywaters and Edith Thompson* (Notable British Trials Series, 1923), edited by Filson Young. William Hodge and Co. Ltd, and London Express News and Feature Services, 1923.

Letters of Violet Trefusis from *Violet Trefusis: A Biography*, copyright © 1976 Philippe Julian and John Phillips, Methuen Ltd. Reprinted by permission of Harcourt Brace and Company.

Letter of Marina Tsvetayeva from *Letters: Summer 1926* by Boris Pasternak, Marina Tsvetayeva and Rainer Maria Rilke, translated by Margaret Wettlin, Harcourt Brace and Company. Reprinted by permission the publisher, Jonathan Cape Ltd.

Letter of 'Vanessa' to Swift, from *Vanessa and Her Correspondence with Jonathan Swift*, edited by Martin Freeman, 1921, published by Hutchinson Ltd.

Letters of Edith Wharton from *The Letters of Edith Wharton*, edited by

R.W.B. Lewis and Nancy Lewis, published by Simon & Schuster. Reprinted by permission.

Letters of Virginia Woolf. Copyright © the Estate of Virginia Woolf.

Letter of Mary Wordsworth from *Love Letters of William and Mary Wordsworth*, edited by Beth Darlington. Reprinted by permission the editor and the publisher, Chatto & Windus Ltd.

Letters of Mary Wollstonecraft from *Letters to Imlay* C Kegan, 1879.

INDEX